F✦:✦RHS
Friends of ROSE HILL station

Supplied via FoRHS
after use.
Please support our

A BOY FROM SIKLIS

By the same author:

FICTION

Seasons of Flight
The Tutor of History
Tilled Earth: Stories

NON-FICTION

Forget Kathmandu: An Elegy for Democracy
Mustang Bhot in Fragments
The Lives We Have Lost: Essays and Opinions on Nepal

A Boy from Siklis

The Life and Times of Chandra Gurung

MANJUSHREE THAPA

ALEPH

ALEPH

ALEPH BOOK COMPANY
An independent publishing firm
promoted by **Rupa Publications India**

Published in 2013 by
Aleph Book Company
7/16 Ansari Road, Daryaganj
New Delhi 110002

Copyright © Manjushree Thapa 2009, 2013
Photographs courtesy the Chandra Gurung Conservation Foundation

First published in India by Penguin Books India 2009

All rights reserved.

No part of this publication may be reproduced, transmitted, or stored in a retrieval system, in any form or by any means, without permission in writing from Aleph Book Company.

ISBN: 978-93-82277-50-7

1 3 5 7 9 10 8 6 4 2

For sale in South Asia (Bangladesh, Bhutan, India, the Maldives, Nepal, Pakistan and Sri Lanka) only.

Typeset in Bembo Roman by SÜRYA, New Delhi

Printed and bound in India by
Thomson Press India Ltd., Faridabad

This book is sold subject to the condition that it shall not, by way of trade or otherwise, be lent, resold, hired out, or otherwise circulated without the publisher's prior consent in any form of binding or cover other than that in which it is published and without a similar condition including this condition being imposed on the subsequent purchaser.

To Barune Thapa, Maya Thapa Ó Faoláin and Siddhant Thapa: Nepal, back in the old days.

I am, it is true, wandering out of place and time. This narrative is faltering. To tell the story of a life one is bound to linger above gravestones where memory blurs and doors can be pushed ajar, but never opened. Listen, or do not listen, it is all the same.
—LOREN EISELEY *ALL THE STRANGE HOURS*

CONTENTS

11   A Dream Come True
20   The Chances of Survival Were Slim
30   Kanchha Mukhiya
43   Once in Fifty Years
53   Kumar Chandraprasad
64   To Become a Big Person
75   He Came Back a Hippie
84   He Hypnotized People
96   Royal Patronage
110   The Accidental Environmentalist
121   The Best Thing in My Life
136   It Was the Association with the Royal Family
148   The Bewilderment Years
165   Vindication
181   A House in Kathmandu
191   Biophilia
206   After the Storm
217   Acknowledgements

A DREAM COME TRUE

To write a biography is to trace a person's afterlife, to feel out how the person lives, still, in the people and places affected by his or her having been alive. For me—who once worked for Chandra Gurung, and whose life was changed by him—it has been moving to encounter him again and again while writing this biography. Here he is, a child in the memories of his family members; there he is, a hitchhiker, a hippie, in the tall tales of his friends; and there he is again, flexing his professional muscles by hosting a glittery gala...We come into this world, and while being shaped by our milieu we shape it as well, leaving behind an imprint, deep or shallow. Few leave an imprint as lasting as Chandra's.

Yet this biography has also entailed a hard lesson in mortality, for there was to Chandra the charmed quality of a man endowed with great good luck, a man who got the impossible done—anyhow, on the fly, adventuresomely, often in pell-mell fashion, but always with success. His boyish, can-do spirit was summarized by the Nepali expression bhaihaalchha: of course it'll happen. The September 2006 helicopter crash that ended his life, and the lives of twenty-three others, laid bare the incaution with which he lived. Yet, through the shock of his death there was an eerie feel of completion to his life. Just one day before the crash, he had overseen the government's handover of the Kangchanjunga area, in Nepal's eastern hills, to the people of the area. This was the first such handover in the country, a milestone in conservation history. All of Chandra's work had led up to it. It was as though he had only just completed his life's work before dying.

'It must have been because he had such a short time to live that he always worked so hard,' was how his elder sister Humkali put it to me in her home in Pokhara town many months later. She was weepy, still having difficulty accepting that her brother was gone. 'That must be why he was always in such a hurry to get so much work done,' she said. 'He had only a short time to live.'

On the morning of 22 September 2006, Chandra was doing what he loved best: gearing up to mark yet another professional success. He headed the World Wildlife Fund Nepal, which oversaw the Kangchanjunga Conservation Area Project, called KCAP in short, in the remote eastern hills. Chandra's previous work, particularly in his native Annapurna area, in west Nepal, had proved that it was the people of any given area, rather than government officials and bureaucrats in far-off Kathmandu, who best promoted nature conservation. We take care of what we feel is ours: that is, apparently, human. At the urging of environmentalists, the government had thus far allowed local people to *manage* their forests; but now, in Kangchanjunga, they were going to grant the local people full *ownership* of their forests. This marked a democratic breakthrough in the country's not-so-democratic history of conservation. The handover was history in the making.

WWF Nepal had, accordingly, spared little expense,

chartering a helicopter to take staff and dignitaries, both national and international, to Taplejung bazaar, the headquarters of the eponymous district where the ceremony was to take place. The passengers gathered at Kathmandu's domestic airport that morning. A micro-manager driven to do everything properly, Chandra had spent weeks planning out every detail of the trip. Though it was just an overnight trip, he had, typically, packed it with activities. The ceremony was to take place that afternoon, followed by festivities at night. The following morning, there would be a quick helicopter trip to a village called Ghunsa. It was in Chandra's style to mark the handover not just in the district centre—a relatively affluent town—but in a forgotten village as well. The programme in Ghunsa would take no more than half an hour. The itinerary would put everyone back in Kathmandu the following afternoon, well in time for him and the WWF staff to prepare for an annual award ceremony scheduled for a few days later and for a staff retreat the following week.

The passengers that morning included some of the people Chandra most respected professionally, some of the people he was closest to personally. Dr Harka Gurung was a geographer by training and a policymaker by calling, a man who had literally shaped Nepal, having helped to delineate its internal boundaries. He was an adviser to WWF Nepal, and a close friend and mentor to Chandra.

Mingma Norbu Sherpa oversaw WWF's programmes in Nepal from its US office. A soft-spoken, methodical man, he was quite unlike the garrulous Chandra; yet the two had often worked together, forming a uniquely complementary team over their intertwined careers. They had jointly established the Annapurna Conservation Area Project—ACAP being the predecessor to KCAP, and the foundation on which KCAP's work was built. Mingma had been a lifelong protector to Chandra, creating professional openings for him and even housing him, for years, in an apartment in his Kathmandu home. He had headed WWF Nepal before Chandra, vacating his job for him, not for the first time.

Just as close to Chandra was Dr Tirtha Man Maskey who had launched his career in conservation as the first warden of Nepal's first national park, the Royal Chitwan National Park, and had retired as the director general of the government's Department of National Parks and Wildlife Conservation. It was for his insider's knowledge on government that Chandra most turned to him, setting him up in a room in the WWF Nepal office building from where he co-chaired the Rhino Specialist Group for the International Union for the Conservation of Nature.

Many others had been invited to the handover ceremony, including the minister of state for forests and soil conservation, Gopal Rai, a local from the eastern hills who happened to be in his constituency at the time. The plan was for the helicopter to pick him up on the way to Taplejung. His wife, Meena Rai, was at the airport for the helicopter ride. Other government officials there included the acting secretary of the Ministry of Forestry and Soil Conservation, Damodar Prasad Parajuli; the Director General of the Department of Wildlife, Narayan Prasad Paudel; and the director general of the Department of Forests, Sarad Kumar Rai. Environmentalists considered all three to be key allies in the government. Vijaya Shrestha from the Federation of Nepalese Chambers of

Commerce and Industries was there from the private sector. Margaret Alexander and Dr Binjan Acharya, of the United States Agency for International Development, were present as donors. The chargé d'affaires of Finland, Pauli Antero Mustonen, was also there as a donor, as a friend of Chandra and—having been part of the negotiations over the Kyoto Protocol—as an environmentalist.

Most of the remaining passengers were WWF staff. The Canadian Jennifer Headley and the Swiss/Australian Jillian Bowling Schlaepfer were from WWF UK. Ghana Shyam Gurung (Ghurmet) and Neera Pradhan Shrestha were with WWF Nepal. Nepal Television's journalist Hem Raj Bhandari and cameraman Sunil Singh were there to cover the ceremony. The helicopter, a Russian craft, was owned by Shree Airlines. Captains Valeri Slafronov and Mingma Sherpa were piloting the helicopter, and crew members Klim Kim and Guruwar Tandual were manning it.

Bad weather delayed the flight. The monsoon had yet to taper off that September; it was cloudy in the hills, and visibility was dismal. Neera Pradhan Shrestha had not known till the previous night whether she would be going on this trip: she and Jennifer Headley had joked that she might have to cut-and-paste her face on to the photographs that Jennifer brought back. The pioneering Nepali environmentalist Hemanta Mishra, or the tourism entrepreneur Karna Shakya, was supposed go in her stead. When they both bowed out at the last minute, Chandra had telephoned Neera, telling her to pack. She was glad for the chance to go. It would be her first visit to the Kangchanjunga region.

Talking to me months afterwards in the WWF Nepal office in Kathmandu, Neera said that Chandra was jaunty and upbeat that morning. When their flight was finally announced, he warned everyone to go to the toilet before boarding: 'There are no toilets on the helicopter!' Neera was the last to go to the toilet. Chandra waited for her, and they got on the helicopter together.

Poor weather prevented the pilots from landing where they had arranged to pick up the minister. Instead they landed at the army barracks in Okhaldhunga bazaar, a full five hours' walk away. The minister made his way there on foot, while the rest of the team went into Okhaldhunga bazaar for lunch. Neera described the hills as slippery, and the day as hazy, drizzled by rain. The Finnish chargé d'affaires had to buy new shoes just to negotiate the muddy trails. Mingma Norbu Sherpa, who had grown up in the eastern hills, took everyone to a lodge called the Solukhumbu Hotel, where they had masu-bhat: meat and rice. The team members wandered the bazaar afterwards. Jill Bowling bought a few souvenirs. At one point Chandra placed a telephone call to the WWF office in Kathmandu. He sounded frustrated about the delay, but still excited about the ceremony.

It was late afternoon when the minister reached Okhaldhunga bazaar and the plans could resume at last. The handover ceremony was quite delayed by then. Nevertheless, as the helicopter approached the plains of Phungling, near Taplejung bazaar, the passengers on board saw hordes of local people waiting to greet them.

Ang Phuri Sherpa of WWF Nepal, who had headed KCAP for four years, was among those waiting in the crowd. He had come a week earlier to prepare for the handover ceremony. 'For Dr Sah'b'—this was what those who worked for Chandra called him—'this was the culmination of the work he had begun in ACAP, twenty years back,' Ang Phuri explained to me later, at the WWF Nepal office in Kathmandu. It had taken nine years to reach the point of handover, he said. At first, the KCAP staff had been uncertain about whether the local people were ready to take on ownership of the forests. (They wanted to see the local people become conservation-minded first.) Then there had been delays from the government. Only when Gopal Rai—a local—became minister of state had the path cleared. The people of the area were as excited as WWF about the handover. 'From the village level, from the district level—everyone important was there that day,' Ang Phuri recalled.

As Neera saw it from the helicopter, the entire hillside of Phungling was coloured bright by the dress of the people who had gathered to greet them. The festive mood was infectious. It was a ten-minute walk from the helipad to the hall where the ceremony was to take place. Dawa Tshering Sherpa, the chairperson of the local council of 'the people' to whom the area was being handed over, led the way. More than a thousand people were packed into the hall. Harka Gurung lost his eyeglasses in the melee. The delay in arriving meant that the original plan to welcome the team with a meal had been scrapped. 'Neera, take pictures,' Chandra said, pressing his camera into her hands just as the ceremonies began.

'They were very powerful,' said WWF's Ghana Shyam Gurung (Ghurmet) of the speeches that marked the ceremony. Having worked as KCAP's first manager, Ghana was particularly attached to the project. He told me that district representatives of all eight national political parties praised the handover—no mean feat, considering that their ideological affiliations swung from conservative to Maoist. Jill Bowling saluted the women of Kangchanjunga in her speech. Ghana said that Chandra looked extremely pleased during the ceremony. Chandra was an exceptionally good-looking man: tall, with a dark, handsome face and a dimpled smile. He was radiant during Dawa Tshering Sherpa's speech in praise of the handover.

'For Dr Sah'b it was a dream come true,' said Ang Phuri. Ghana agreed: 'This was the culmination of his life's work.' The ceremonial part of the programme involved the lighting of a lamp, and the offering of Tibetan scarves, khatas, and flower garlands all around—even to a peepal or bodhi tree. At eight, with all the formalities completed, the guests were fed at last: sel-roti, or rice-flour sweets, and rice pudding and potatoes.

Dinner had been prepared at the Taplejung City Hall, a further ten minutes' walk away. Tungba, a specially brewed millet beer that had been fermented for over three months, was served that night. There was no shortage of merrymaking in the programmes that Chandra had put together. After dinner, traditional dance troupes staged dances of the local Sherpa and Limbu nationalities. Then Chandra broke out in a folk song, seemingly spontaneously (for this was a staple of all his programmes; in anticipation, KCAP staff had invited local guitarists to dinner). The song Chandra sang that night was his favourite, 'Sohra barsa umeramaa', about a lusty old man lamenting his lost youth and virility. Enthused by the success of the ceremony—conservation history!—and by the warm welcome of the local people, the entire team took part in the singing and dancing.

Chandra never entirely lost himself in such merrymaking, though. For him this was just part of doing things properly; his style was to mix the serious and the difficult with the light and the celebratory. At the end of the night he did not forget to pay the necessary dues. The singing and dancing ended around 10.30 p.m. Jennifer Headley, Jill Bowling, Harka Gurung, Neera and Chandra were staying in one lodge. The rest of the team had other accommodation. Ang Phuri told me, 'Afterwards, Dr Sah'b came to where we were. He thanked me personally.' In a society where the bosses tend to claim the credit for any success,Chandra was very generous to his junior staff: Prajana Waiba Pradhan, his assistant at WWF, told me that he never ended a single workday without thanking her. For Ang Phuri, who had spent years working for this handover, the event had been an immense professional accomplishment. It was gratifying to have Chandra acknowledge this publicly.

THE CHANCES OF SURVIVAL WERE SLIM

The next morning, on the way back from Ghunsa village, the helicopter crashed, killing everyone on board. Our knowledge of this crystallizes our view of the morning's events and imbues the smallest gestures with import.

Neera Pradhan Shrestha was scheduled to go to Ghunsa, and she prepared accordingly. Before the flight, Chandra took everyone into Taplejung bazaar with the promise of some 'special' coffee—which turned out to be just Nescafé with foam. The weather was inconstant, with grey clouds lowering over the hills. Over coffee, Ang Phuri Sherpa asked the pilots whether they would be able to take off. 'We must,' replied Captain Valerie Slafronov. There was some confusion about who would be going. Though the helicopter had a twenty-four-passenger capacity, it was not advisable to have more than seventeen or eighteen passengers in the thin high-altitude air. Yugaleshwar Thakur, a local forest ranger, was supposed to go, but Dawa Tshering Sherpa took his place. Nepal TV journalist Hem Raj Bhandari had said he would not go, but at the last minute he changed his mind. When Vijaya Shrestha also decided to go, Neera was left behind. The passengers boarded. The helicopter took off at about 9.30 a.m. The weather was fickle. Ang Phuri felt uneasy watching the helicopter take off.

Ghunsa was a fifteen-minute flight through a gorge that narrowed in one place, then widened again. The programme there was to last no more than half an hour. The helicopter would then return to Taplejung bazaar, landing either at Phungling, or, depending on weather conditions, at another plain in Sukhetar, a two-hour walk away, to take everyone back to Kathmandu.

The programme in Ghunsa took place without incident. We know that those on board, as well as the WWF staff who had gone ahead to make preparations, were met with garlands by the villagers. Yeshi Choden Lama was one such staff. She was described by all her WWF Nepal colleagues as extremely dedicated. The American Matthew Preece was also in Ghunsa, having come from WWF US. The villagers offered everyone tea and snacks, and an interaction programme followed. Afterwards, some celebratory singing took place; but without too much tarrying, the twenty-four return passengers—now including Yeshi Choden Lama and Matthew Preece—readied to leave.

All helicopter flights rely on visibility; the pilots must check the view out of the cockpit window against topographical maps. After the helicopter took off, WWF staff in Taplejung bazaar received a telephone call from Ghunsa confirming its departure. When, half an hour later, it had not reached Taplejung bazaar, Ghana Shyam Gurung (Ghurmet) called WWF's office in Kathmandu to report the delay. Forty-five minutes later, at around 11.30 a.m., the helicopter had still not arrived. WWF staff in Taplejung bazaar tried not to worry—till a radio message came in from Kathmandu: Shree Airlines had confirmed that the craft was missing.

Then came a second, more distressing call from Ghunsa. People there had heard explosions soon after takeoff—first a small bang, then a bigger bang. They had not seen anything through the clouds, but the sounds had been those of explosions.

The mood in Taplejung bazaar darkened. 'We didn't say so, but we immediately figured that the chances of survival were slim,' Ang Phuri told me. He had gathered with Ghana and other WWF staff. Neera, who had gone to wait at the house of a local staff member, grew alarmed when people around her started to cry. Everyone tried to focus on finding out what had happened, but their efforts were hampered by poor communications. They wanted to put through a conference call to the office in Kathmandu, but—so nationally renowned were those on board, news of the accident was already spreading—all the telephone lines to Taplejung bazaar were jammed. Anxious family members were calling directly to find out what had happened. Kathmandu's news media, and its intellectual and NGO circles were already abuzz with word of the missing helicopter, and also with conjecture and speculation, making it difficult to separate rumour from truth. Soon the WWF staff in Taplejung bazaar began to receive calls asking whether it was true that the helicopter had been located after all, and that everyone had been found alive—a rumour that everyone in Kathmandu, including I, had heard by then.

'It took us seven calls to trace the source of that rumour,' recalled Ghana, whose following days, weeks and months were consumed by the accident. 'Naturally, we wanted to know whether there were really any survivors.' Beginning with the person who had phoned with the query, he placed one call after another from Taplejung, eventually tracing the source of the rumour. It turned out that a Kathmandu socialite had said this wishfully at a dinner party; and hope had spread from cell phone to cell phone.

As soon as the helicopter disappeared, the WWF office in Kathmandu went into emergency mode. Anil Manandhar, who was second to Chandra at WWF, found himself overseeing the rescue and recovery of his closest friends and colleagues. Anil remained calm in the face of crisis. He cancelled all existing plans—including the award ceremony that was to have taken place after the trip, and the staff retreat—and set up several teams, delegating to them separate responsibilities. He remained part of a core team that hunkered down in a back room in the office building, making policy decisions. This team was shielded from all but the most essential communications with the authorities, and with the families of those on the helicopter.

In Taplejung bazaar, Ghana and Ang Phuri formed a fact-finding team. As weather delayed the arrival of search-and-rescue helicopters, they phoned Ghunsa, dispatching three search teams to scour the countryside. They then set off by foot for the village.

Neera, stranded in Taplejung without any transportation back, became part of the effort there. A fourth WWF team in Kathmandu was handling phone calls and queries from the public, and briefing visitors who had begun to drop by the office in hope of news.

The weather remained dismal over the following days.

Several helicopters were on stand-by, but none could fly into the area. By the 24th, one of the search teams that Ghana and Ang Phuri had dispatched from Ghunsa had sighted the helicopter on the side of a 4,000-metre cliff in a place called Gyabla. Ghana and Ang Phuri met the search team in the village of Phale, en route to Ghunsa. The team had not been able to reach the helicopter, which lay in an inaccessible niche. They discussed the possibility of reaching it using yaks and ropes, and that night they walked together to Ghunsa.

Only on the following morning—the 25th—were they able to get some professional help. Five experts from the Nepal Mountaineering Association and the Himalayan Rescue Association Nepal flew into Ghunsa on an army helicopter, equipped with gear. 'We, of course, didn't know any of the technicalities involved in such operations,' Ang Phuri said to me. The experts did. They led the way.

It took four hours of climbing from the village and bushwhacking through the outlying wilderness for the team to reach the bottom of the cliff against which the helicopter had crashed. Only those with professional climbing skills could reach the crash site. No one was found to have survived. The need for rescue became moot. The bodies could not be recovered without more manpower and equipment. That day, the team only took photographs and left.

Early on the 26th, a team of fifteen to twenty local people, with a much larger network of secondary helpers, began the difficult work of recovering the bodies. By then the families of those who had perished were desperate, as were their circles of friends, acquaintances and well-wishers around the country, and indeed the world. Matthew Preece's sister had arrived from the US. Other family members who had been abroad, including Chandra's daughter, Amanda, and Harka Gurung's children, studying in the US, were en route. The government announced a day of national mourning. All this placed immense pressure on the recovery effort. The secretary of the Ministry of Culture, Tourism and Civil Aviation, Madhav Ghimire, exchanged heated words over the slow pace of the recovery with Ang Kaji Sherpa of the Nepal Mountaineering Association. Yet the terrain was just too inaccessible; there was no way of speeding up the work.

The people of Ghunsa, and of the neighbouring Lelep and Phale villages, were extremely upset about what had happened, and they aided the recovery effort. Ang Phuri said, 'They fed us even at two at night; they constantly offered us tea and raksi; they covered the bodies with their own blankets.' Neera, still stranded in Taplejung bazaar, was in shock at how those she had been with just days before were now being called 'the bodies'. Before leaving the bazaar she had to identify their bags, which they had left behind in Taplejung. There were Hindu scriptures on top of Narayan Prasad Paudel's suitcase, she told me. 'I knew Narayan Sir was religious, but when I saw that—' Many months later, Neera still found it difficult to talk about the accident. 'Jennifer was so warm, she was always ready to help others,' she said. 'She had a...godly character. Yeshi was so quiet, yet so powerful, so dedicated...And Narayan Sir—on the way to Taplejung, he and I had talked about how many of his family members were doctors and engineers...' Everyone was still so vivid in her mind.

Sudden, accidental death leaves people grasping for resolution. Everyone I spoke to about the accident was left trying to summarize a whole person through fragmented memories. 'He paid attention to the smallest people, he never treated anyone unequally,' people said of Chandra. Of Yeshi Choden Lama: 'She was always so serious—but when she laughed, the whole building shook!' The Finnish chargé d'affaires Pauli Mustonen was hosting a concert by the modern Nepali singer Aavaas upon his return. 'He had phoned up everyone before the trip, reminding them to come,' said Juho Uusihakala at the Embassy of Finland. 'Jennifer was always smiling,' WWF Nepal staff told me. And: 'It was Mingma who always helped Chandra advance.' 'Harka Gurung took the most meticulous notes. Even on field trips, he was always taking notes, comparing them with those he had taken years before...'

It took till the 27th to bring the bodies back to Kathmandu. There was another delay in returning them to the families; this could take place only on the following day. Funeral rites began at once, the families of the deceased observing a variety of Hindu, Buddhist and Christian rituals, as per their faiths.

In Chandra's case, there was a bit of confusion as to how to organize the funeral. He was long estranged from his first wife, Sumitra Manandhar Gurung. His second wife, Tokiko Sato, lived in Jordan, and was herself hospitalized with back problems at the time. Both his parents had passed away some years earlier. His elder sister Humkali lived in the town of Pokhara; his eldest brother, Chitrabahadur, lived in their birth village, Siklis; and his other brother Totraman lived in Boston. In the first few days after the accident there was no one to even host visitors to Chandra's house in Kathmandu. The caretaker did not have enough money to buy tea or biscuits.

His nephews and nieces, colleagues and friends all pitched in. They asked his first wife, Sumitra Manandhar Gurung, to host visitors to his house, and she did so, graciously. By then their daughter, Amanda, had returned from the US, interrupting her college year. Their son, Adhish, had been by his mother's side throughout. Chandra's eldest son, Yoichi—whose mother was Tokiko Sato, Chandra's second wife—flew into Kathmandu on the 29th, just in time to light his father's pyre at the funeral ghats of the Pashupati temple. This was the first time Yoichi had met his half-siblings, Amanda and Adhish. Chandra's youngest son, Eiki, remained with his mother, Tokiko Sato, in Jordan. Chandra's last rites were performed in strict adherence to Gurung custom, with local pajyu and khebri—shamans—and all the food, meat and alcohol brought from Chandra's birth village.

After the funerals came the memorial services. Every institution affiliated to the deceased—literally hundreds, all over the country—held services in their memory, up to three or four a day for weeks on end. For months afterwards, people went about Kathmandu weepy, crying at the slightest trigger. I confess I was among them. Immediately after college in the US, I had worked for Chandra during what I had thought would be a brief stay in Nepal; but he had made me decide to stay on, to live here. Though we had lost touch in recent years, I had always thought we would reconnect one day. Harka Gurung, too, had been a close family friend: I remembered him from early childhood on. I had fond memories of Mingma Norbu Sherpa, telling me, almost fifteen years earlier, in the village of Ghandruk, in the Annapurna foothills, that J. R. R. Tolkien had trekked through the area and based the Hobbits' forest on the rhododendron forests there.

And even the loss of those I had not known felt personal, for Kathmandu's is a small society, where social circles intersect extensively. Everyone I knew knew someone who had died in the accident. Also, Nepal is the kind of country where very few individuals know how to cut through the prevailing dysfunction to get things done. So many of those on board were known for just this. They were the best the country had. Between them, the Nepalis alone had five PhDs, and degrees from the University of Hawaii and the University of Florida in the United States; the Asian Institute of Technology in Thailand; Patna College in India; the University of Edinburgh and the School of Oriental and African Studies in the United Kingdom; the University of Canterbury in New Zealand; Leiden University from the Netherlands—and, of course, a variety of colleges and the Tribhuvan University in Nepal. Each life had been such an investment. The accident seemed an utter, utter waste.

Yet the work at WWF Nepal—which had lost its leader, as well as so many staff and national and international allies— barely skipped a beat. None of the Kathmandu-based staff, or the field staff—scattered from the country's eastern to western borders, through the plains and up the hills and mountains—took any time off. Anil Manandhar, who went on to head the organization, deliberately chose this to be the case: 'It seemed worse to sit around and remember the people we had lost,' he told me almost a year later in his office room. I had got to know Anil nearly a decade earlier, when we had both worked for Chandra at ACAP. He had always been steadfast, implacable. The decision to keep working seemed remarkable to me. But perhaps there was compassion in it. 'Everyone was close to breaking down, everyone was always crying,' he explained to me. 'It seemed more constructive to carry on with work, to keep the organization strong.'

There was, perhaps, a psychological need for everyone to focus on something other than on grief—and work became the most obvious alternative. And, objectively speaking, there was a lot of work to do. Five days after the accident, WWF held a memorial programme, offering a stricken Kathmandu society a way to grieve collectively.

Soon after, all the WWF programmes that had been cancelled were rescheduled, one by one. The conservation award was given, that year, to an all-women's group. The cancelled staff retreat was never held; but other programmes continued. Yet grief over lost friends and colleagues—and the shock of personal mortality—lingered in the office for many months, finding expression when the staff talked among themselves, or when they discussed the accident with outsiders like me. 'We all tried our best to keep going,' was how Neera put it to me a year later. 'We were all so worried that our work would suffer, so we tried very, very hard. We tried so hard. But sometimes, it was as though we were all just pretending to work.'

KANCHHA MUKHIYA

First there is the land, then there is the matter of what we do with it. Nepal lies along the geologically turbulent collision line of the Indian plateau and the Eurasian continent, a collision line that stretches from Pakistan in the west to Burma in the east. The earth is said to be 4.6 billion years old. About 150 or 200 million years ago, two tectonic plates, Gondwanaland and Laurasia, got detached from the Pangaea landmass and broke further, forming the continents as they are today. Upon the division of the Indo-Australian plate, the Indian plate drifted north at 26 centimetres a year, considered very rapid by geological standards. Even after its collision with Eurasia, 70 million years ago, this drift has continued at 4 millimetres a year, still considered rapid. Nepal, at their meeting point, is still active with the dip-slips and strike-slips, creep zones and locked zones: it is a volatile, earthquake-prone land.

The Swiss geologist Toni Hagen has hypothesized that the physical formation of the land here took place over four periods. The first occurred with the collision of the tectonic plates, the displacement of the Himalayan Sea that had been in between them and—as the Indian plateau slid under the Eurasian continent—the up-thrust of the loose, terraced seabed that formed the Tibetan marginal mountains. Today, these mountains lie just where the himals (as Nepalis call all snow-capped mountains) meet the Tibetan plateau. The Churia range, comprising Nepal's southernmost hills, was also formed at this time: it consists of debris deposited by the rivers created by the collision.

This collision took place in the presence of life. Long before the Indian plate began its northward drift, the formation of complex molecules—sugars, nucleic acids and amino acids—had begun in the seas. Upon the formation of DNA, these molecules had evolved into varied and increasingly complex life forms. Bacteria had come into being, feeding on hydrogen through photosynthesis. Then blue-green algae had developed, feeding on sulphur and producing, as a by-product, the oxygen we now depend on. Protisia, or multi-celled cooperative communities, followed; then came sponges, thriving in vast, complex colonies. By the time the Indian plate reached Eurasia, life had evolved beyond micro-organisms. Trilobites, sea creatures—the first creatures endowed with sight—had already gone extinct. Among the flora, there were mosses and ferns, conifers and cycads and flowering plants. Fauna, including multi-cellular animals with nervous systems, covered the seas and the land: molluscs, fish, amphibians, worms, reptiles, mammals, insects and birds. In Nepal's unstable, seismically active soil, not much remains of the most ancient life forms, save for ammonites. Worshipped by Hindus as manifestations of Vishnu, ammonites are the fossils of marine life from the Himalayan Sea. They are found now in the exposed riverbeds of the Tibetan marginal mountains, and are for sale in the tourist stalls of Kathmandu.

The second period in the physical formation of the land

took place ten to sixteen million years ago, when immense, rocky massifs squeezed up from the Indian plate, up to 4,000 metres. This was the first appearance of the himals. The Tibetan plateau rose higher than the himals at the time, up to 6,000 metres. The rivers changed course with these upheavals, the force of their water flow breaking through the mountains to create the north-south transverse gorges that still crisscross the land today.

The third period in Nepal's physical formation started 700,000 years ago, and continued through the period of Homo erectus, the two-legged hunter, toolmaker and communicator that was Homo sapiens' predecessor. In an especially violent reaction to the compression of the two tectonic plates, the rock sheets of the himals squeezed upward in this period, gaining a further 3,000 metres in height. All the 8,000-plus metre summits of the himals were formed at this time. So rapidly did they rise that the rivers that flowed from them were trapped, damming as high valley lakes. This, the period of the first ice age, also saw the formation of the first glaciers.

In the final period, 200,000 years ago, the himals slipped back down, and the land settled into its present contours, with three major north-south transverse gorges (at the three main rivers: Karnali, Narayani and Koshi) and seven distinct east-west geological zones within the borders of present-day Nepal.

From north to south these geological zones are: the Tibetan marginal mountains, rising to 7,000 metres, but remaining arid, without snow or glaciers, and with the loose, terraced soil of the seabed it had once been. Then there are the Inner Himalayas, the high valleys immediately north of the himals. These valleys include Thak Khola—the only one to fall on a north-south transverse gorge—and Humla, Mugu, Langu, Manang, Kutang, Kyirong, Rongshar, Khumbu and Karma. The Himalayas themselves comprise the third geological zone, rocky and mostly uninhabitable, with extreme altitude variations between the low valleys and the high summits. (The Kali Gandaki gorge that cuts between Dhaulagiri and the Annapurnas is a stark example of this.) The midlands come next, a narrow strip divided by transverse gorges into nine areas: Chamlia in the west, and moving eastward, Seti, Karnali, Bheri, Kali Gandaki, Trisuli, Sun Kosi, Arun and Tamur. The soil in these areas favours farming. (Kathmandu valley—once famed for the fertility of its soil—falls in the midlands.) South of the midlands, running west to east over the breadth of Nepal, is the fifth geological zone, the Mahabharat range, with low valleys and mountains of uniform metamorphic rocks as high as 3,000 metres. The Churia range, immediately south, constitutes the sixth geological zone: hills of alternating soft and hard strata which rise out of the Gangetic plains, up to 2,000 metres. In places these hills merge into the Mahabharat range; in Chitwan, Rapti and Dang, they form low-lying valleys. Finally, south of the Churia range is the tarai, an alluvial stretch of the Gangetic plains, which is just sixty metres above sea level at its lowest point.

Siklis village lies at the foothills of the Annapurna himals, in the midlands. It is the highest of Nepal's Gurung villages. Compared to the country's remotest villages, it is not impossible to get to, but neither is it easy. From Pokhara you must find a ride north-east along rough tracks washed away, in unpredictable cycles, by floods in the Modi River. No one except the locals can tell you how far the track goes in any given year. Eventually you reach the village of Swonda. From there begins a steep climb uphill, a six-hour climb punctuated by a single tea shop. The villages of Parche and Khilang come into view, but Siklis remains out of sight till the very top of the hill. Even then, you have to walk more than an hour to reach the village.

Like most Gurung villages, Siklis consists of a huddle of stone houses surrounded by terraced fields. It is not the prettiest of the area's villages. The houses here boast tin, rather than slate, roofs; the terraced fields are sparse and the rhododendron forests and alpine pasture lands beyond are blocked from immediate sight. There is no view of the himals. Still, when I went there to see Chandra's birthplace, I was moved by the air of dilapidated pride that the village wears, its air of having withstood the influences of the outside world.

Of course it has not. Talk to anyone, and you quickly hear of family members in Pokhara and other cities in Nepal, or abroad—in India or Hong Kong or Korea or Japan, or farther afield: in the United Kingdom, Europe, the United States. The Gurungs have long served as Gurkha soldiers in the British army, and as Gorkha soldiers in the Indian army. Lahurey is the Nepali term for these soldiers, the term arising from the city of Lahore, in present-day Pakistan, from where

Nepali soldiers were first recruited to the army of Maharaja Ranjit Singh. Recruitment into the British army began after Nepal's defeat by the British East India Company in the war of 1814–16. The lahurey tradition continues till today. Of Nepal's ninety-odd castes and janajatis—ethnic/indigenous nationalities—the Gurungs are now among the better-off because of the earnings of the lahureys.

This affluence has translated only gradually into prominence on the national stage. Since its formation in 1768, the Nepali state has been all but monopolized by the Hindu 'high'-caste groups: the warrior-caste Chettris, including the Ranas and the Shahs, who have claimed the right to rule; and the priest-caste Bahuns, who have used their hold over the Nepali language, and over religious learning, to control bureaucracy, education, media and politics. The indigenous Newars of Kathmandu valley have cooperated with these two castes, if sometimes reluctantly, by offering cultural sanction. On this narrow stage there has been little space for the ethnic/indigenous janajatis or the so-called low-caste groups, the Dalits.

However, with the rise of multiple civil rights movements following democracy in 1990, things have been changing. The movement for janajati rights is one of the many civil rights movements under way in Nepal, along with movements for women's rights, Dalits' rights, the rights of Madheshis (inhabitants of south-east Nepal), gay and lesbian rights, and the rights of the differently abled. The janajati rights movement has focused on cultural rights—the right to run schools in mother tongues—and the reclamation of lost, or suppressed, identities. The Gurungs have taken the lead in this movement.

Indeed, most Gurung activists no longer call themselves Gurung, preferring the indigenous term 'Tamu'. The Tamu Dhi is the most prominent of their organizations.

Chandra was born in 1949 to Ratansingh and Krishnakumari Gurung, the sixth of seven children. Ratansingh was the kro or (in Nepali) mukhiya—headman—of Siklis village. There are traditionally four 'high' Gurung clans, known as the four-jaat Gurungs, as well as sixteen 'lesser' clans, known as the sixteen-jaat Gurungs. The family belonged to a 'high' clan, the Gothane clan; and, as was the case with most mukhiya families, had some link with Kathmandu, the centre of state power.

The family was endowed with a sense of its history. Ratansingh's father, Narsingh Gurung, had been the mukhiya of Siklis before him, the last mukhiya to exercise full power. Narsingh had a serious speech defect, but he was strong. According to local lore, he had no trouble at all lifting the mukhyauli dhungo, or village headman's rock, which stood in his courtyard as a symbol of his status. It usually took two men to lift the rock. However, because of his speech defect, Narsingh was not able to earn. As a consequence, he had to send his son Ratansingh to Kathmandu to work for a well-placed relative, Kali Bahadur Subedar.

At the time, Kathmandu was an arduous week's walk away. Serving Kali Bahadur Subedar, Ratansingh learned how to read and write, but he was not happy. He once tried to join the army, going to the military grounds of Tundikhel to see if he could enlist. Lacking permission from his employer, he was turned away with a stern reprimand. Still he looked for an escape. This he found after lending money to a gambler in a game of kauda, or cowrie shells, during the autumn festival of Tihar. The gambler had been losing, but his fortunes turned with Ratansingh's money. He repaid Ratansingh generously out of his winnings.

With this money Ratansingh walked all the way back to Siklis, or at least he tried to. He contracted malaria on the way, and ended up at the house of a Bahun-caste mit, a ritual friend, near Pokhara. When they learned of his illness, the villagers of Siklis came to his mit's house to fetch him. Back in the village, Ratansingh established himself as a man of learning, an intellectual: he was the only man lettered enough to write official deeds and letters. The mantle of mukhiya eventually passed from his father to him.

Chandra's mother, Krishnakumari, was also lettered, a rarity in her time. The daughter of a colonel, she was quiet by temperament, but well versed in the Hindu scriptures. She could give sermons on the Ramayan and the Mahabharat, and knew how to conduct even the most intricate religious rituals. She was also skilled in astrology and soothsaying, and she taught her husband these arts.

I found the family home in the neighbourhood of Dhaprang, in Siklis, looking down on the rest of the village. It was identical to all the other village houses: the walls were of stone, with a slanting roof that would once have been of slate, but was now of tin. (It was a sign of Ratansingh's prosperity that he could have the corrugated tin sheets carried in from the town of Butwal.) Maize and chilli peppers hung out of the wood-frame windows above a stone-paved courtyard. With Ratansingh and Krishnakumari both gone, the house had an abandoned air. Inside, on the ground floor, was a single room with a sunken hearth. Upstairs was another room that used to be the main bedroom. The house was not showy. The walls were bare, with only a few family photographs on a shelf. One was of Chandra and his father: Ratansingh small and wizened with age, and Chandra, tall and strapping, both men dressed in kachhads, the white wrap that is part of Gurung men's traditional dress.

In his youth Ratansingh had been a powerful man, ruling over his raiti—the villagers in his charge—the way a king rules over his subjects. 'The old man was a real dictator,' was how someone who knew him put it to me, not without affection. The villagers turned to the mukhiya when they needed disputes settled, or when they needed advice. Traditionally, the mukhiya had also raised taxes for the state, but by Ratansingh's time this was no longer the case. What made him especially popular in the village was his skill in astrology and soothsaying.

Ratansingh and Krishnakumari were a far-sighted couple, determined to prepare their sons for more than soldiering as lahureys, and their daughters for more than marriage. Yet they were also products of their time.

Their first daughter, Reshami, and the third daughter, now remembered only as 'Sainli', or 'third daughter', both died very young, leaving behind hardly any trace.

Humkali, their second daughter, did not study. She married Ganga Bahadur Gurung of neighbouring Khilang village, and now lived with her husband in Pokhara. Their nine children were scattered from Siklis to Pokhara to Kathmandu and farther: the United Kingdom, Japan, Singapore.

Ratansingh and Krishnakumari's fourth child was a son, Chitrabahadur. From a young age Chitrabahadur showed little interest in following in his father's footsteps to become the village mukhiya. Perhaps because he was hard of hearing, he was not keen on studying either; and try as they might, his parents could not motivate him. Chitrabahadur still lived in Siklis, very much a village man, overseeing the family fields and herding the cattle to the pastures. His ten children—by his wife Sunmaya and by three other women—were scattered in Siklis, Khilang, Ghandruk village, Pokhara, Kathmandu and Belgium.

The family's second son, Totraman, proved far more ambitious. He was now a PhD, living in Boston with his American wife, Erica, and three children from his previous wife, Chijmaya, who remained in Siklis.

Laxmi, the youngest child and the family's fourth daughter, broke all village bounds by studying nursing. She was pursuing her studies in Kathmandu when she contracted tuberculosis and died in a tragedy that scarred the entire family.

Before her, though, there was Chandra. By Gurung custom, children are birthed in the mother's maternal home, where the mother is pampered with massages of warm ghiu (clarified butter) and cared for by traditional midwives. Childbirth is a cause for celebration. Rice beer, chhaang, is fermented and aged for months preceding the birth. Afterwards, the mother is fed the meat of a female chick, to strengthen her bones. The father's family sends over ghiu and rice, and a rooster or, if possible, a goat.

Upon Chandra's birth, Ratansingh feasted all of Siklis. An announcement was sent around by word of mouth, granting the birth social recognition. Children are named after three days, following their first bath, and adorned with ritual threads. A jyotish, astrologer, determines the child's name. Chandra's full name was Chandraprasad, the Bahun-caste suffix indicating his parents' aspirations to education, to learning. In the family, Chandra was known simply as Kanchha, or youngest son. To the villagers he was Kanchha Mukhiya, the youngest son of the village headman.

His sister Humkali told me that Chandra wore silver bracelets on his wrists and ankles till the age of five. 'He cut his foot in Khilang once, and Father carried him all the way back,' she recalled. Chandra was the darling of the family, and extraordinarily attached to his father. (Even as an adult, he shared his father's bed when visiting the village.) More than his brothers, Chandra took pride in being a headman's son. 'He was very astute,' Humkali told me, 'always telling our father: so-and-so did this, so-and-so said that. He used to advise Father on who were friends and who were foes, and get him to invite our "own people" to the house.' She smiled at the memory. 'The old village grandfathers used to say, if he's like this as a child, imagine what he's going to be like as an adult!'

Humkali was already an adolescent when Chandra was a boy. Totraman and Chandra were close, she said, but of quite opposite temperaments. While Totraman was introverted, Chandra was an extrovert. While Totraman was finicky, Chandra was adaptable. 'My second brother wouldn't eat just any food,' sister Humkali said. 'But Kanchha, he was never bothered about good or bad; he would eat anything.'

Chandra was not without the usual streak of prankishness,

but his parents were intent on making him—and his siblings—'big persons': important people, thulo manchhe. 'You must grow up to be a big person' is a common exhortation of upwardly mobile parents throughout Nepal. When Chandra was caught playing truant one day, skipping school to play a game called ampui, his father had his hands tied, and forced him to study.

And study he did, though I found accounts varying as to whether or not he was brilliant. He was quick to grasp information, and he did apply himself. Perhaps most decisively, he had his parents' ambition to drive him.
Down the way from Chandra's family home lived a childhood friend of his. I went to meet him during my stay in Siklis, to gather his memories from their boyhood. The friend was dressed in a kachaad, his sun-burned face bearing witness to a life spent toiling outdoors. Polite, even diffident, he sat me down on a stool in their stone-paved courtyard. The morning air was wintry, but the sun was bright. A vista of inky-blue mountains loomed beyond.
He told me that he and Chandra—whom he called Chandraprasad—had learned their letters together in the village school: 'There was a small school above the tailor's house, a school that went up to class three.' The school was rudimentary, without accreditation. 'It was opened by a man named Bahadur Gurung, a lahurey, one of those old men who had retired,' he said. The learning there was all by rote. 'There was no such thing as an exam. There'd be the papers that the schoolmaster would look at. As for the students, we had to learn to recite everything by memory. The schoolmaster would look at the papers, and we had to recite everything out loud. Only then

would we pass.' He laughed. 'We memorized entire books that way!'

To supplement this learning, Chandra's parents hired a private tutor for him and Totraman. 'They got a Bahun to come to the house—a master who couldn't pronounce "ra", and said "la, la", instead,' their sister Humkali told me. Chandra quickly caught up with his brother. He always found his brother's books more interesting than his own, Humkali said. 'He picked up everything so fast.'

When the brothers passed out of the village school, their parents decided to send them to Pokhara, to attend a proper school. Chandra's childhood friend gave me a sense of what a departure this was from the norm.

'Me, I studied till class three,' he said. 'I don't understand Sanskrit, but I do understand Nepali—just by studying till class three. After that…if my father had encouraged me, I might have studied, too, but… My father was a simpleton.' He frowned, earnest. 'Now Chandraprasad's father was clever. My father only cared about raising buffaloes, cows, sheep.' Such were the prevailing values of village life, he explained. 'To be prosperous in the village meant having buffaloes, cows and sheep. Without all three you had no respectability. If you produced everything you needed—that's what it meant to be prosperous, then.'

Ratansingh and Krishnakumari wanted their children to enjoy more than just local respectability, he said. 'Chandraprasad's father even came to my house and told my old man, look, our sons are friends, let's send them down to Pokhara together. But my old man? He said, "If my sons go down there, they'll get malaria and die." So Chandraprasad went to Pokhara, and I went off to the pastures, to herd cows.' He laughed.

ONCE IN FIFTY YEARS

As I was talking to Chandra's childhood friend, his thirty-something son joined us where we were sitting. In contrast to the father's kachaad, the son wore Western clothes. His bearing was modern, and his manners less diffident.

Together, father and son gave me a sense of what life in the village used to be like, and of the changes it had undergone over the years. As someone who had spent his whole life farming, Chandra's friend was part of a waning generation. He acknowledged this wistfully: 'Who'd put in all the work to live in a village now?'

Most villagers found it necessary to leave—if they wanted to escape a life of toil, that is. For them, Pokhara was the most obvious alternative. About 200 families from Siklis had already settled there, the son told me: 'That's just counting the families who are part of the samaaj.' The samaaj—the society—was a formal network whose members contributed money towards cultural events and community projects. Of course, some families chose to live outside the society's bonds, he said. Still, they tended to remain in Pokhara. Not many families settled in Kathmandu. Those who ventured beyond Pokhara just went abroad, he said.

'The income is better abroad, if you work for a few years, like me—' He explained that he had just returned from

Korea. 'I mean, forget my father's time,' he said, frankly. 'Even when I was growing up, there wasn't a high school here.' Like Chandra, he had gone to Pokhara to study. Afterwards, he had wanted to join the British Gurkhas, or the Indian Gorkhas; but the competition had proved too stiff. 'Instead, I decided to go to Korea. And I did. And I earned quite a bit,' he said, with a touch of pride. Two of his brothers were in France, one of them a member of the Foreign Legion. Neither was likely to return to Nepal, or to Siklis, except for family visits. He himself, it turned out, was only here contemplating his next move.

I sympathized with his desire to leave—and also with his lingering attachment to home, to family. Siklis, which falls outside the Annapurna area's major trekking routes, has no lodges to employ the youth, no work to keep them from leaving the village. Out of curiosity, I asked the father and son what alternative there was to leaving. Was there any way to earn a proper living in the village?

'There's been no attempt to do so, so it's hard to say that it's not possible,' the father answered, though his vagueness alone seemed telling. The son named fruit and vegetable farming as options, but he sounded unconvinced. They both immediately said that the lack of road access posed a serious obstacle to developing the village. Three years earlier, the very year it was built, the road to Swonda village had been washed away by the Modi River. The societies of Siklis, Khilang and Parche villages had paid for its reconstruction. 'It wasn't as though the government gave anything; the people raised the money: sixty-two hundred thousand or thereabouts. That's what it cost,' the father told me. 'Something happened at the river's headwater, the snow melted, there was a flood.'

'Now everyone's afraid that the same thing will happen if they rebuild it,' his son added.

In addition to the road, the water supply also needed improving. 'There's a source, we all share the water, but it could be improved,' the father said. As for ways to earn a living, however, neither they nor I could think of many alternatives...

Our talk eventually meandered back to Chandra. His life had changed completely after he went to Pokhara to study. The father had last met him upon Ratansingh's death, when Chandra had come to attend his father's arghau, a ceremony to mark a death. The entire village had been feasted at Ratansingh's arghau. 'Of course we didn't get to talk much,' his friend said to me. 'It's a time of sorrow. And...' Though they had gone to the same school as children, a certain distance had come between them afterwards. 'He didn't come here a lot—I suppose he didn't get much time off. And after the Maoists put his name on the list, we couldn't really tell him to come,' he said.

What list, I asked.

'Eh, "he engaged in corruption," that kind of list,' he said evasively.

'Nonsense, all nonsense,' his son said.

I discovered that until just a month before my visit, Siklis had been under occupation by the Communist Party of Nepal (Maoist). The Maoist leaders Pushpa Kamal Dahal 'Prachanda' and Baburam Bhattarai had lived here under the protection of their People's Liberation Army through the summer of 2006. This, after joining forces with the democratic political parties to end King Gyanendra Shah's absolute rule in April 2006. Peace talks had been launched. The Maoists had moved into Siklis for the duration. The interim minister of home affairs, Krishna Prasad Sitaula, had even flown into the village in a helicopter to finalize the Comprehensive Peace Accord. Then, in November 2006, just a month before my visit to Siklis, Pushpa Kamal Dahal 'Prachanda' had walked down from the village, in dramatic style, to sign the accord in Kathmandu, an accord that marked the end of a ten-year civil war. Siklis had been intimately linked to national politics throughout this period. But to look at the village just a month later, you would not know it at all.

From the father and son I learned that, during their occupation of the village, the Maoists had targeted Chandra's family especially. All over the country, the Maoists had seized the land of 'feudals': their stated class enemies. In a village like this, the mukhiya's family made for an obvious target. The Maoists were also distrustful of ACAP, the conservation project that Chandra had launched in this area, since its parent organization, the King Mahendra Trust for Nature Conservation, had been patronized and chaired by the royal family. In their anti-monarchy zeal, the Maoists accused Chandra—of all things—of smuggling dried venison and precious herbs to the royal palace, and of helping to suppress the April 2006 movement against King Gyanendra's rule. Someone even filed a suit against him at the Centre for the Investigation of Abuse of Authority in Kathmandu.

Ratansingh and Krishnakumari were long dead by then; the family house was lying vacant. When the Maoists threatened to take it over, though, the villagers rallied back. 'We went to the Maoists,' the father told me, 'and we talked to one of their big people, a district-level person. We said, "What has Chandraprasad done? If the people of the village say he's done something wrong, then you can go against him. But no one has said anything. You can't do just anything you want."'

In the end the Maoists spared the family home; and the suit filed against Chandra came to nothing. I found it ironic that Chandra—who had, at ACAP, so wanted to help 'his people'—should have been tarred in such a way. Were there any Maoists here whom I might talk to, I asked.

There were not. They had all left upon the signing of the peace accord. 'It's been a while now,' the son told me. 'Sometimes one or two of them come by, but it's never one of the higher-ups. It's only the useless ones who hang around now.'

But weren't any of the Maoists originally from Siklis, I asked.

He shook his head no. 'There wasn't even one person from here. They were all outsiders. And whatever they said, we had to do. There's no one from this area. Not one. If you go downhill, to the Bahun villages, you'd find some Maoists there, maybe. But not here.'

I soon took leave of the father and son, and went to see the ACAP office, along a leafy incline. Even before occupying Siklis, the Maoists had forced ACAP to halt all work here. In the village of Ghandruk, they had bombed ACAP's headquarters, leaving it in ruins. Here, the building stood intact, elegant and stately, of traditional stone and slate, but with clean modern lines. Chandra had commissioned the design himself. The

Maoists, who had occupied the building during the peace process, had put up hammer-and-sickle graffiti on the walls, and slogans warning: Danger!

Now vacated, the building housed a day care centre that ACAP had started, a programme that had proved popular among the village women, as it freed them to do more productive work. The centre was now run independently by a local mothers' group. I peeked into one of the classrooms and saw children seated on benches in straggly rows, chanting the alphabet out loud. The woman who ran the day care centre came out to talk. She had known Chandra well. She told me he had been a great promoter of mothers' groups.

I remembered this from my time at ACAP. The mothers' groups too had been extremely fond of Chandra. The woman who ran the day care centre recalled with particular admiration how very local Chandra was. 'You know, he spoke our own language with us,' she said to me. 'Not just Gurung-bhasa, but the tongue of this village. He'd speak our tongue with us, and he'd speak Nepali with government officials, and he'd speak English with foreigners—all perfectly. Most of us—even our educated people—they mix everything up, they don't even remember their own tongue. Not him. But then, he wasn't just anyone. A man like him,' she said, 'comes around only once in fifty years.'

She showed me around the office grounds. A statue of

Chandra stood at the front, a recent addition. The previous day, Chandra's first wife, Sumitra Manandhar Gurung, had come to the village with their daughter, Amanda. Amanda had placed a colour photograph of her father near the office gate. ACAP's old nursery remained in the grounds: people could buy saplings for their tree plantations, eliminating the need to collect firewood or fodder from the outlying forests. The greenery in Siklis, the woman told me, was because of Chandra. 'He encouraged us to plant all this'—she pointed at the lush broadleaf trees that shaded the main path through the village—'otherwise it was all bare.' The stone trails of the village had been paved at ACAP's behest, and private toilets built with its help. ACAP had supported the launch of a community-run tourist lodge; though with very few trekkers coming through Siklis, it was not used much any more. Of course, ACAP had not turned around the village's fortune— its mandate was not for economic development, it was just a conservation organization, after all—but it had done what it could to ease the arduousness of village life.

The Maoists had closed ACAP, but its presence lingered, I saw. I felt Chandra's imprint everywhere, and the imprint of his family. Beyond the office gate was a school where Chandra's Boston-based brother Totraman once used to teach, and which he had helped turn into a middle school. ACAP had subsequently expanded it into a high school: the children of the village no longer had to go to Pokhara to study. One of the local schoolteachers, Suresh Gurung—called 'Suresh Sir' by the villagers—passed by as I stood at the office gate, looking out at the blue mountains. We had met the previous night, at Chandra's family home. Now we waved in greeting; then I watched him walk on.

I found Siklis moribund without ACAP. Chandra had once infused the Annapurna area with his boyish, can-do bhaihaalchha spirit. Now everything felt stagnant. Of course everything is temporary; everything passes. The emptiness of Chandra's family home was a stark reminder of this. Chandra's family—his eldest brother, Chitrabahadur, and his wife, Sunmaya, their son Lokraj and other members of the extended family—had been very hospitable to me, housing and feeding me in the Gurung way, opening their homes to me. I was especially thankful for the company of Lokraj. Though he was a quiet man, he harboured strong feelings for his uncle, for ACAP and for the changes the village had gone through; and this had generated an unspoken affinity between us. This made me feel the absence of Chandra more acutely.

Leaving Siklis, I took an alternative route back to Pokhara, along a high ridge, through the village of Ghale Gaon. The Ghales are descendants of ancient Gurung kings, and, according to local lore, the ancestors of the 'high' four-jaat Gurungs. I wanted to see one of their settlements. And I had wanted to walk this route for years: ACAP had developed it to promote 'eco-trekking'—low-impact trekking—and the beauty of its old-growth rhododendron forest was legendary.

It was grey and misty on the morning that I headed out. My partner Daniel was along for the hike. A wiry village elder led us past an alpine pasture, through a green, rolling vale. Above the village, the sounds of human habitation fell away, and the wind whistled in the pine trees as we passed the turn-offs to the neighbouring villages. The mists shifted and swirled as we walked. In the high pastures, we could hear an occasional tinkling of bells, and the calls of faraway cowherds. Soon we crossed a waterfall along a lichen-covered rock face, and entered the rhododendron forest.

It was dense there, and dark, the light filtering through the leaves tinged green. The air smelled of dirt and dampness, of rot and regeneration. The tree trunks were covered with moss, and mushrooms bloomed on the ground; from somewhere came the harrumph of an animal we could not see.

I did not generally get the time—or make the time—to get to the natural world much, though I do harbour a vague, romantic 'love of nature'. Rachel Carson, the 'mother' of the environmental movement, has been kind about this vague love in *A Sense of Wonder*: 'Once the emotions have been aroused—a sense of the beautiful, the excitement of the new and the unknown, a feeling of sympathy, pity, admiration or love—then we wish for knowledge about the object of our emotional response. Once found, it has lasting meaning.' I wondered whether, in writing Chandra's biography, I might have such emotions aroused, and then move beyond emotion, into knowledge.

The trail through the forest wound up across a high ridge, then down along a saddle, then up again. Had the day been clear we might have seen the himals from the ridge. But the mist only thickened as we walked. Soon it started to rain. There was nothing to do but keep walking; this was what we did. Eventually we reached a clearing where, many years earlier, ACAP had built a house and toilets—a campsite for trekkers, so that they would not have to clear the forests to erect their tents. Few trekking groups came this way now, but the house was still there. It was derelict, its walls covered with graffiti drawn, apparently, by the Maoists. On one wall was a portrait, in charcoal, of the Maoist leader Baburam Bhattarai giving a speech, an M-16 bordering the portrait.

We took shelter in the eaves of the house as the air grew chilly, and the rain hardened. Silvery hail began to pelt down from the sky. The camp ground was soon covered with a silver sheen. We stood shivering, looking out at the hail storm, and waiting for it to end so that we might be off, for we were still many miles from Ghale Gaon, and we needed to get there before darkness fell.

KUMAR CHANDRAPRASAD

When Totraman and Chandra went to Pokhara for their schooling, Ratansingh sent someone with them—not to show them the way, but to run ahead, clearing ill omens from their path. In later years, recounting this to friends, Chandra would marvel at how much his father had cared for them, how far he had gone to ensure their well-being.

The Pokhara that Chandra and Totraman came to, in the early 1960s, was utterly unlike the bustling town that it has since turned into. It lacked electricity, roads, amenities or infrastructure—and also its present-day sprawl. The bazaar consisted of a single street. No highway connected it to Kathmandu. Pokhara fell, rather, on a north-south axis, acting as a hub for the people of the inner himals—from Mustang, the Thak Khola gorge and Manang—who travelled back and forth between Tibet and India for trade. As in Kathmandu, the Chettri and Bahun castes, and the bazaar's Newars, dominated the state institutions in Pokhara. To highlanders like the Gurungs and Magars of the outlying hills, it was a hot, malarial town from whose administration and governance they were firmly excluded. Pokhara was some place to go to only for a good reason; its attractions were otherwise limited.

The town grew rapidly after 1950, when Nepal set on a mission of nation-building. Before that, the country was sealed off from the world, having diplomatic relations with only India and the United Kingdom. This isolation had suited the maharajas of the Rana clan, who, upon capturing power from the Shah kings in 1849, had harnessed the state's resources to private benefit. In 1950, political activists from the Nepali Congress Party and the Communist Party of Nepal, with the cooperation of the ailing King Tribhuvan Bir Bikram Shah, brought an end to Rana rule, and the start of what was to be a long struggle for democracy in Nepal.

The democratic government launched headlong into modernization. In a world gripped by decolonization, and Marshall Plan-style reconstruction, 'development'—and specifically the development of the Third World through foreign aid—became the call of the day for countries like Nepal. The government expanded education and health programmes, and encouraged small industries to set up all over the country, including in Pokhara. Democracy also helped to break the monopoly of the narrow elite: in Nepal's first general elections of 1959, Min Bahadur Gurung of Pokhara, a member of the Nepali Congress Party, became the first Gurung ever elected to Parliament.

But in 1960, the new king, Mahendra Bir Bikram Shah, effected a coup, reviving his dynasty's absolute rule. The coup was quickly endorsed by India, the United Kingdom, and the rest of the world: in 1961, Queen Elizabeth even paid an official visit to Nepal, sealing the international stamp of approval. For King Mahendra had sold himself as a 'benevolent dictator', arguing that in a Third World country like Nepal, the imperative for development was more urgent than the imperative for democracy. India signalled its endorsement by continuing its aid. The United States—at the height of its period of international do-goodism under John F. Kennedy's leadership, and on the cusp of launching the Peace Corps—continued to support the government through USAID. The Cold War was on. Not to be outdone by the United States, the Soviet Union and China, too, continued aid to Nepal.

The absolute rule that King Mahendra launched—which came to be known as the Panchayat era—brought unprecedented social engineering to Nepal. The country was divided into seventy-five districts, fourteen zones and five development regions; Hinduism was instituted as the state religion; Nepali became the national language; and the state encouraged the migration of hill people to the valleys, and to the plains of the tarai, to promote what was called 'national integration'. (The result, as we have since seen, was the assimilation and subjugation of less powerful castes, ethnic/indigenous and regional groups of the tarai: their internal colonization by the hill people.)

Pokhara grew rapidly during this period as the people of the outlying hills relocated to avail themselves of government services and modern amenities here. The Gurkha pension camp also set up here, enabling retired servicemen to collect their pensions locally, instead of travelling all the way to the town of Gorakhpur, in India, to do so. Lahurey families began to settle in the town, quickly gaining a reputation for their worldliness and affluence. Pokhara's bazaar expanded as business grew. In the 1960s, Nepal found a place on the so-called hippie trail from Europe across the Middle East to India, and a few private lodges were set up on Fewa Lake. Through all this, however, the town remained small by today's standards. The population was less than 5,000 when Chandra and his brother Totraman arrived at the start of the 1960s. Now it is approximately one million.

Pokhara had only two high schools at the time: the Multipurpose National High School and the Soldiers Board Vocational Training High School. Of the two, the latter had higher academic standards. Founded in 1957 with aid from the Indian government to educate the children of Gorkha servicemen, it was known to instil discipline in its all-boys student body. This was the school that Ratansingh had chosen for his sons.

The Soldiers Board Vocational Training High School still stands where it did at that time, though it is much bigger, and has been renamed the Amarsingh High School. I went there to meet the principal, Dr Aiyamma John, to see what she might tell me about Chandra's boyhood there. Past a high gate I entered the school's large, well-laid grounds. The original mud buildings were now dwarfed by new concrete structures stacked several stories high. Beyond the buildings was a sports field that had just been an open plain in Chandra's time. The school had always been run as a non-profit community school. These days it boasted a plus-two curriculum (an extra two years of schooling after the tenth class, when high school ends in Nepal), and separate English and Nepali sections, as well as a section for educating the blind, using Braille.

It was results week when I visited. The principal's office was surrounded by students who had just got their results, and who wanted to say a quick thank-you before ending their school year.

Aiyamma John nevertheless made time to talk to me. She and her husband, George John, were fixtures in Pokhara's recent history: countless 'big' people had passed through their hands at one or another educational institution in the town. Originally from India, they had landed in Pokhara entirely by chance. In 1953, on graduating from Patna University, George John came to Kathmandu: he walked up from the Indian border town of Raxaul. He lived in Kathmandu for a few years, in a flat above a well-known dry-cleaning establishment called My Shop, tutoring during the daytime and studying at night at the Nepal National College. It just so happened that one of his tutees was the brother of the chairman of Pokhara Municipality. The tutee often complained that only four people from the town had ever received a bachelor's degree, and that no one had ever received a master's. He urged George John to help start a college in Pokhara, and persuaded his brother, the municipality chairman, to furnish the necessary certificates and appointment letters.

When George John flew into Pokhara in 1959, the town's airport seconded as a grazing field. He had set up the Prithvi Narayan Campus with thirty students, and had lived in the city ever since. Aiyamma John had shared her husband's journeys both personally and professionally. She gave me a sense of what the Soldiers Board Vocational Training High School had been like when Chandra came here as a boy.

'There used to be more discipline than there is now,' she said, talking to me in Indian-inflected, yet grammatically correct, Nepali. The walls of her office were decked with the awards and trophies that the school had earned over the years. She said, 'The students used to have to salute, army style. They were better behaved than they are now.' But there were more girls now, she noted. She named two early female students who went on to do well—Narayani Mulmi and

Urmila Pant—and talked about how shocked she, who was originally from South India, had been to discover that Nepalis did not bother to educate their daughters. 'Even in the Prithvi Narayan Campus in 1960, there were no lady students,' she exclaimed, still outraged after all these years, 'whereas in South India, even then, for every four or five thousand boy students, there used to be three or four thousand girls. Nepal simply had no custom of educating girls!' she exclaimed. 'Now, it's all girls in the plus-two programme,' she boasted. 'The education sector is all girls.' The school became particularly well regarded when it added a science section. 'Before that,' she said, 'it was possible to get a science education across the Seti River, but not on this side. It was just an ordinary school before that.'

Still, many of its students had earned renown. Harka Gurung had attended the school, as had the founder of the Boy Scouts in Nepal, Heram Koirala. 'Mahesh Gurung also went here,' Aiyamma John said, assuming that I recognized the name, which I didn't. 'And the headmaster of Kalika School'—a well-known Pokhara school—'Balram Chapagain.'

By this time the line of students waiting outside her office had grown very long. I did not want to keep them from ending their school year, so I thanked Aiyamma John. She put me in the hands of a teacher, who, sharing Aiyamma John's pride in the school, showed me through some very well-stocked science labs, none of which would have been there in Chandra's time.

The Matepani neighbourhood of Pokhara, on the town's north-eastern outskirts, lies directly on the route to Siklis. Chandra and Totraman took lodgings here with other schoolboys—including two cousins, Jagman Gurung and Badri Gurung—from the village of Yangjakot. An old woman from Yangjakot looked after the boys cursorily, but for the most part they had to fend for themselves. This began their abrupt transition from pampered mukhiya's sons to ordinary boarders.

Jagman Gurung was not just a cousin, but—as the son of Chandra's paternal aunt—a soaltee. (A soaltee, or, for females, a soalteeni, is the child of a maternal uncle or a paternal aunt; by tradition, Gurung families prefer to marry soaltees above all other matches. There is, accordingly, as another of Chandra's soaltees, Hum Bahadur Gurung, put it to me, a 'certain formality' between soaltees.) Jagman Gurung went on to become a professor at Kathmandu's Tribhuvan University. Talking to me in his home in Kathmandu, in a room decked with Hindu, Buddhist and Bon accoutrements—for he was deeply spiritual—he told me that the boys at the lodgings took turns cooking. Ratansingh did visit his sons, and Chandra and Totraman did go home on the holidays; they got all the rice, beans and ghiu that they needed from home. The lodgings were basic, though. 'There was no electricity, we had to study by lamplight,' Professor Gurung told me. Chandra, he said, was brilliant.

The other cousin, Badri Gurung—the son of Chandra's maternal aunt—disagreed. For many years, Badri ran businesses in Pokhara, including Open House, a popular gazal restaurant in the Chipledhunga neighbourhood. When I met him he ran the Royal Kitchen, one of the largest dance restaurants in Kathmandu. He remembered Chandra as a hard-working student, but one with indifferent results. 'After all, he graduated with third-division marks,' he told me. 'But once he put his mind to anything, he would succeed at it. He worked very hard.'

Both cousins agreed that Chandra was exceptionally gregarious. He took part in all the school's extra-curricular activities. 'Even if he didn't know how, he would sing, he would dance,' said Badri. 'He played badminton, he tried everything. He had no inferiority complex at all.' His disposition was positive: 'Bhaihaalchha, he felt everything was possible.'

I learned that Chandra was also driven, from a young age, to do everything properly. In Pokhara I met Balbir Singh Negi, known to his students as 'Negi Sir'. He had taught Chandra in class nine, and also later in college. He spoke to me of Chandra's perfectionism: 'He would start each page of his writing with "sri"'—a Hindu tradition to signal the auspiciousness of letters—'and when he greeted his teachers, he would join his palms and click his heels together,' he said. 'He had a cultured air. He was different. Refreshing.'

Of the Soldiers Board Vocational Training High School, Negi Sir said, 'It was a novelty at the time, an Indian-style school.' As part of their daily regimen, the boys were required to do military-style march pasts. But they also studied history and geography, and English, maths, science: the curriculum was fully modern, Indian-style. Among their extracurricular activities were dance performances in which the boys had to dress up as girls for all the female roles. The school was strict, and the teachers meted out corporal punishment, he said, quickly clarifying that Chandra was never beaten. Chandra's academic performance, like that of all the boys, was bolstered by the school's own ambitions. 'There was a big push to have a hundred per cent of the students pass,' Negi Sir said. At the insistence of a colonel at the Indian embassy, the teachers ran evening classes, all by lamplight. When the school was first established, a few students would invariably fail each year, and only two or three would pass with first-division marks. He said, 'Later, many began to pass in the first division, and there were even students who came first in board'—with top marks nationwide.

Through primary and middle school, Chandra was known as Kumar Chandraprasad—kumar, which literally means virgin, being an indicator of childhood. He dropped the childish affix on reaching high school. He was already tall by then: in a few rare photographs from the time he is painfully thin, all long bones. Unusually, he was endowed with a sense of self, and proud of his roots, constantly exhorting Negi Sir: 'Come to my village, Sir. You must come. But don't come in the month of Chaitra: there are hailstorms if outsiders come in Chaitra.' Negi Sir told me that though during school hours Chandra wore ordinary clothes—Western-style shirts and pants—when attending evening classes he would put on a bhangra, a cloth that crisscrosses the torso, serving as a catch-all in Gurung men's traditional dress. 'It's my mother, my culture, that gives me my identity,' was what he said Chandra used to say in school. In an era of assimilation, this was an exceptionally assertive statement coming from a young Gurung boy.

Now, with the rise of the janajati rights movement, there is renewed debate as to what constitutes Gurung—Tamu—

culture, with many Gurungs eschewing Hindu customs. Chandra's soaltee, Professor Jagman Gurung, told me that by Chandra's time, so assimilated were the Tamu into the culture of the Chettri and Bahun caste elite that it was difficult to separate 'pure' practices from the mixed practices any more. Ratansingh and Krishnakumari belonged to a generation that deferred to Hinduism. Later generations, including today's janajati rights activists, have taken up Buddhism. But according to Professor Gurung, the Tamu people were originally neither Hindu nor Buddhist, but Bon, animist.

He explained that when the Rana maharajas framed Nepal's first civil code in 1854, they created a hierarchy of four groups: the 'high' Hindu castes, the unenslaveable alcohol-drinkers, the enslaveable alcohol-drinkers and the 'untouchable' Hindu castes. The Gurungs adopted Hindu customs to escape being classified as 'enslaveable' alcohol-drinkers, a misfortune that befell other groups such as the Bhotes, Kumals, Chepangs, Tharus and Ghartis. The legacy of this assimilation remains to this day. Professor Gurung said, 'Some families use a Bahun puret for rituals; other use a Buddhist lama; others use Bon pajyu and khebri.'

Ratansingh's family was typically mixed up. They turned to pajyu and khebri—shamans—for their ritual needs, yet they observed Hindu and Buddhist festivals alike. In Siklis, as Professor Gurung explained, the calendar year started in the middle of what we think of as winter, with Lhosar, and the Pusé Pandhra festival. This was followed by the worship of the wind, or Bayu puja, in the springtime, during which it was customary to stage a recital of the Hindu scripture, the Chandi. Later in the spring came the celebration of Buddha

Purnima, on the full moon marking the Buddha's enlightenment. In the late spring came Dashara, celebrated for peace and prosperity. Sauné Sankranti, in the summer, entailed ancestor worship. Then came Dashain and Tihar—the most prominent Hindu festivals—in the autumn, or harvest time. Chandra grew up with this eclectic mix of Hinduism, Buddhism and Bon; and till the end of his life he had an ecumenical approach. Hinduism, Buddhism, Bon: all were his heritage.

TO BECOME A BIG PERSON

As Chandra passed from adolescence to adulthood, he faced the question of what to do, who to become—how to become a 'big person'. This, in a country in formation, where the possibilities were endless—yet the precedents were few. Conservation did not exist as a subject of study at the time; it likely never occurred to Chandra to enter the field. Studying beyond high school was itself unusual; for the common pressure in Gurung society was to pursue fortune, rather than fame. Gurkha recruitment—becoming a lahurey—was an obvious option. His sister Humkali told me that the village elders of Siklis often asked their father whether Chandra and Totraman weren't going to try out for the Gurkhas. 'My father always said, "No, my sons will never do lahurey work,"' Humkali told me, echoing her father's adamancy. Being a soldier—even a highly paid one—was dangerous work, after all. 'He didn't want his sons to suffer. He didn't want them to have to follow others' orders, or risk bullets, or tramp around in jungles. He would say, "I'm going to educate my sons, and turn them into big people."'

Chandra did explore the option, though. He accompanied Humkali's husband, Ganga Bahadur Gurung, when he went to try out as a lahurey. But unwilling to disappoint his father—'What would Ba say?'—he decided against trying out.

Thaman Bahadur Gurung, originally from Khilang village, was Chandra's classmate in high school, as well as a soaltee. I met him at Humkali's home, where he told me about this formative juncture in his and Chandra's lives.

Just as Ratansingh wanted Chandra to study, Thaman Bahadur's father, himself a British Gurkha serviceman, wanted his son to obtain at least a bachelor's degree. After high school, both he and Chandra decided to study science. There was no science faculty at the recently opened Prithvi Narayan Campus in Pokhara. So they travelled together to Kathmandu to take an entrance exam at the Trichandra Campus. In Kathmandu they stayed in the apartment of a common family acquaintance, a man who worked as a health post in-charge. When the results of the entrance exam were announced, their names were not on the list.

Chandra immediately returned to Pokhara and enrolled at the Prithvi Narayan Campus, where his brother Totraman was already studying. In so doing he abandoned science and took up geography. Thaman Bahadur discovered that he had passed the entrance exam after all, but—lacking the company of a friend—he decided against enrolling that year.

'I never thought I'd become a soldier,' he said to me, musing over the haphazard way they had both made life choices at that age. By the time Thaman Bahadur returned to Pokhara, it was too late to enrol at the Prithvi Narayan Campus, so he went home to Khilang village. It was recruitment season in the village. The Gurkha recruiter, locally called a galla, had set up camp in nearby Swonda. 'All the boys were going to show themselves to the galla,' Thaman Bahadur told me, laughing. He joined them on a whim.

'There were about a thousand or twelve hundred, or maybe two thousand, boys.' They had come from the outlying villages. 'None of them had passed out of school.' The recruiter measured their height and their chest, and gave chits to those who were sufficiently well-built. (The rest returned home disappointed.) A family friend who was helping out with the recruitment recognized Thaman Bahadur. 'What are you doing here, son? Coming to get recruited?' He ordered the galla to measure him, whereupon Thaman Bahadur was given a chit and told to report to Pokhara in a week.

'There were no roads in Pokhara then, you had to walk all the way to the airport to get weighed,' he explained. Most of the applicants were eliminated at this stage. The one hundred or 150 remaining men had to walk three days to Bhairahawa town, to a camp in a place called Pakhlep, for the next stage of trials. There were daily flights from Pokhara to Bhairahawa at that time, with tickets costing twenty-eight rupees. Thaman Bahadur shared the cost of the galla's flight, and they spent four days in Bhairahawa, waiting for the others to arrive.

In the end, about seventy or eighty boys were recruited, including Thaman Bahadur. Only three of the twenty-two boys who tried out from Khilang village had been selected. Inducted into the Royal Corps of Signals, he trained in the jungles of Malaysia, and went on to serve in Singapore, Hong Kong, Brunei and the United Kingdom, retiring, twenty-one years later, as a Warrant Officer II.

Of Chandra, Thaman Bahadur said, 'We had been like brothers in school. Then—he studied, I joined the army.' Despite their divergent paths they had stayed in touch, meeting at their high school's fiftieth anniversary, when Chandra gave a speech. They had also met after that in Kathmandu. 'I was there to pick up a passport, and I stopped by his office at the World Wildlife Fund,' Thaman Bahadur told me. 'He came to the reception room, and took me to his office. He asked what I wanted to eat, momo or chau-chau. He said he hadn't eaten either. He was like that,' he said. 'He called me his friend, we spoke in our own tongue—he had that village way of speaking, always saying au, au,' He laughed. 'We talked about what we always did, when we met. We talked about the old days.'

Retiring from the Prithvi Narayan Campus in 1995, George John had become principal of the private Gandaki Boarding School, across the Seti River gorge. Chandra's sister Humkali's son, Krishnaman Gurung, took me there to meet him. George John's office looked out on to the well-tended school grounds. Outside the window it was raining heavily.

There was hardly anything to the PN Campus when Chandra enrolled, George John told me. 'Pokhara was a village then, it was all fields, only fields. The airport had to be cleared of cows before the planes could land.' He had opened the campus with just thirty students, but, with expansion in mind, he had insisted that three hundred ropanis, or about thirty-eight acres, be set aside for future expansion. This was possible then, as Pokhara was thinly settled. 'We ran classes out of huts,' he said, laughing. 'I had to teach English, economics and political science myself.' It was registered, at the start, as a community college, with faculties only in the arts and the humanities. 'We had to raise money ourselves to pay the teachers' salaries!'

The college was constantly growing. About 250 students

were enrolled by the time Chandra joined; when he graduated, there were 400. (Now there are 12,000.) The geography department, in which Chandra enrolled, had been opened entirely by chance.

In 1962, when the Peace Corps began to send volunteers to Nepal, the college put in a request for teachers in physics and mathematics, George John told me. 'We wanted to open departments in these fields.' The Peace Corps had obliged; and the physics and mathematics departments were promptly set up. Then the college decided to open a chemistry department. They asked the Peace Corps to send a chemistry teacher, but when the teacher, Peter Farquhar, arrived, it turned out that he was not a chemist, but a geographer. 'He was just a boy, twenty-two or twenty-three!' George John exclaimed. Nevertheless, he was set on the task of opening the geography department.

Chandra enrolled a few years later. The department had only two teachers. One was a Nepali geographer, Dr Madhav Prasad Tripathi, and the other was an American geographer, Dorothy Mierow, a Peace Corps volunteer. Part of the first batch of Peace Corps volunteers in Nepal, Dorothy Mierow had gone to Tribhuvan University, in Kathmandu, before trading places with young Peter Farquhar.

The atmosphere at the campus was extremely informal, George John said. Everyone knew everyone, everything was genial. 'Everything was so—innocent,' he remarked. He gave me a telling example of this. Chandra took his intermediate exams in 1969. 'After the exams in the morning, we would stack up all the answer copies, and just leave them there,' George John said. 'If we caught anyone cheating, we'd just tell them, politely, to leave.' He laughed. 'Now, there were some boys from Kathmandu that year. They had come to observe. They felt that cheaters should be expelled at once. They came to talk to me about this.' George John had not agreed with them; and in anger, they had retaliated. 'There were no grills in the exam-room windows,' he explained. 'They took the answer copies and just tossed them out the window.' Chandra's answer copy was among them. The exams weren't redone that year. All the students had to repeat a year.

Of course this upset them, he said. 'There were protests, yes. We used to live in straw huts on the campus, and they said they'd set them on fire. But in the end the boys'—the observers—'returned to Kathmandu, and the matter died down.' Chandra retook the exams the following year, and passed.

Had Chandra been a good student, I asked.

'He was above average,' George John replied, 'but he wasn't brilliant. I think his marks were in the second division. Yes, second division. Not higher than that.'

What Chandra was not learning in class, though, he was making up for outside, in a rapidly modernizing Pokhara. Being the son of a mukhiya, a village headman, meant little by way of wealth: Chandra had to work his way through college. His first job—straight out of high school—was as an office clerk of a low rank, ironically enough called mukhiya. In 1965, the Department of Cooperatives opened an office in Pokhara to aid the establishment of cooperatives, particularly in cash-crop farming and animal rearing. Govinda Ranjitkar, who headed the office, told me that it was very small. 'The top posts—inspector, auditor and subba—were filled by officials from Kathmandu,' he said, talking to me about this in his house in Kathmandu. The rest of the staff were to be hired locally: a khardar with a monthly salary of Rs 120; two mukhiyas with salaries of Rs 75; a baidar with a salary of Rs 55; and two peons and a guard, a chowkidar, with salaries of Rs 45 each.

Chandra saw the advertisement and applied for a job. 'He came to the interview wearing shorts,' laughed Govinda. 'He was just a boy—he couldn't have been more than sixteen.'

Once hired as a mukhiya, Chandra set to typing documents, sending and receiving letters, and organizing office files. He used to study in the mornings and come to the office at 2 p.m. 'He was a simple boy, very straightforward,' said Govinda, who followed Chandra's progress during his own career in government. He mused, 'Even then, he was always pleasant, always smiling.' The office was in the Matepani neighbourhood, where Chandra still lodged. Govinda visited his lodgings sometimes. 'His father used to come from the village every now and again. I never saw his mother.'

As a Kathmandu native, Govinda found life in Pokhara trying: 'There were no vegetables—it was that undeveloped,' he remarked. By the time he left Pokhara in 1969, Chandra had been promoted to khardar. The Department of Cooperatives not only lent money to new cooperatives, it helped them keep accounts. As a khardar, Chandra kept the office accounts and paid the staff salaries.

Chandra quit the Department of Cooperatives when he was hired as a librarian at the PN Campus. He left his lodgings in

Matepani and moved in with his brother, who was now living on campus with the lecturer and librarian Birendrasingh Gurung. 'There was nothing to the campus, no housing quarters or anything,' Birendrasingh told me over tea at Pokhara's lakeside Fewa Lodge. The hut they lived in had a stone-and-mud foundation and bhakaris—bamboo matting—for walls and flooring. Pokhara was electrified in 1970; but kerosene lamps were still a common form of lighting.

To Birendrasingh, who was born in present-day Pakistan, who grew up in Dharamsala, India, and who returned to Nepal only after completing his education, Chandra seemed very much a 'village boy', relaxed and easy-going to the point of fecklessness. 'He didn't take anything seriously,' was how Birendrasingh put it to me. 'He was always saying tomorrow, tomorrow: leaving things to the last minute.' But Chandra did excel at making friends. 'I don't know how close he ever became with anyone, though,' Birendrasingh commented. An inordinate number of these friends were female. 'During the Tihar festival, for bhai teeka'—a ritual between brothers and sisters—'he had so many sisters—thousands and thousands!'

Two British volunteers, Michael Battye and John Welsh, taught English at the PN Campus then: their friendship lasted all their lives. Chandra's grasp of English increased with such friendships, Birendrasingh said. There was also a foreign 'air hostess' working as a medical volunteer. 'Everyone said they were going to get married,' he laughed.

By the 1970s, the tourism industry had set up for good in Pokhara. In Kathmandu, the Russian ballet dancer Boris Lissanevitch had opened the Royal Hotel in the 1950s. The 1959 ascent of Mt. Everest by Edmund Hillary and Tenzing

Norgay Sherpa had brought international attention to Nepal. By the 1970s, the country had become a must-go destination for travellers and seekers journeying overland from Europe on the 'hippie trail' to Turkey, Iran, Afghanistan, Pakistan, India. While many of these travellers confined themselves to Kathmandu, the more adventurous went farther afield in search of lost worlds, and the mythical Shangri-la. Tales of the abominable snowman, the yeti, drew tourists to the mountains in particular. The British Jimmy Roberts—Colonel James O. M. Roberts—had helped to popularize trekking through his agency, Mountain Travels. In Pokhara, low-budget lodges had appeared along the shores of Fewa Lake. Western anthropologists were also descending on the land by then, avidly recording Nepal's many 'pristine, unchanged' cultures, and arguing for their preservation. In no small part did they perpetuate the country's image as a happy, innocent, lost world.

Chandra's generation was the first in Nepal to be influenced by western youth culture. Information about the sexual revolution, feminism, anti-war movements, be-ins and love-ins, psychedelic and folk music concerts would have all filtered in in bits and pieces, exotic and tantalizing, if not quite attainable. It was common to see hippies swimming naked in Fewa Lake. Notions such as free love, dropping out of society, seeking wisdom in eastern religions and expanding the mind through drugs—Nepal's ganja was world famous, after all—would have swirled around Chandra's milieu. At the same time, as Birendrasingh Gurung told me, for Nepalis inhabiting a more staid society, there was very little to do for fun, other than to go on outings and picnics: 'There were just friends, there was merrymaking,' he said. 'That's all there was.'

Still, Chandra was touched by the era's adventuresome spirit. One winter vacation, he and Birendrasingh decided to bicycle the full length of the newly constructed Kathmandu-Pokhara highway. 'There were very few bicycles in Pokhara then,' Birendrasingh said. Chandra borrowed one from a friend, and Birendrasingh borrowed one from the Peace Corps volunteer Dorothy Mierow: 'A lady's bicycle, an ordinary one, with no gears.' He laughed. They took the bus to Kathmandu. 'It was Christmas time. Chandra stayed with some friends, I stayed with my brother. Just after the new year, we bicycled back.' The ride was 200 kilometres long. It took two days to get back to Pokhara, with an overnight stay in the highway town of Mugling.

Through all this, Chandra retained a close connection to Siklis. He and his brother Totraman returned there on their vacations, often bringing along friends, Nepali and foreign. One Maghe Sankranti, Birendrasingh went along. This winter festival, held on what was considered the coldest day of the year, was observed with a two-day village fair. 'There were people playing shotput, thelo,' he said. 'Everything started at the mukhiya's house, and afterwards, the mukhiya would tie a turban on the winner's head.' From there they went to the nearby village of Tangting, where there was a rodi going on. Rodi is a Gurung custom—now largely lost—of getting marriageable young men and women together for singing and dancing, and for matchmaking. 'Boys and girls would meet, they would sing,' mused Birendrasingh. 'There was a craze for cigarettes at the time. The boys and girls would give each other cigarettes.'

Chandra also travelled to other parts of Nepal on field excursions organized by the geography department. It seems he took up the ethos of nation-building, to go to villages to carry out research, conduct camps, do good, help the needy, serve the poor...

The question of what to do—how to become a big person—arose once again as Chandra neared graduation. Could he become a big person? A boy from Siklis. He joined the Electricity Department in the modest post of a nayab subba.

HE CAME BACK A HIPPIE

It was Dorothy Mierow who changed Chandra's life forever, who helped him break out of Pokhara, into the world. The two had become acquainted while Chandra was working at the library, which occupied a room in the natural history museum of the PN Campus. Though she taught geography, Dorothy cared foremost about the museum. It was her life's mission.

Dorothy's was a sweet story, the story of a Peace Corps volunteer who fell in love with Nepal and made it her second home. She was in her forties when she joined the Peace Corps. Before that, she had taught at Colorado College—where her father served as the president. She had curated the college's natural history museum in Colorado. In Pokhara she had dreamed of establishing a similar museum. She had even put her own family fund into doing so. For it turned out that when he retired her father left her shares worth ten thousand dollars, earmarked for her children, children she never had. She invested that money in the children of Pokhara—by opening a natural history museum.

George John described Dorothy as 'extremely dedicated'. In his office at the Gandaki Boarding School, he told me that there was a big rock called the 'Bhim dhunga' on the PN Campus grounds. Legend had it that Bhim, the brawniest of the four Pandav brothers in the Mahabharat, used to play marbles with this rock. 'Dorothy Mierow decided to build a museum around it,' he said.

To do so, she kept extending her tenure with the Peace Corps. 'I'm not sure she would have stayed on if the museum hadn't been there,' Birendrasingh Gurung told me. About Chandra's friendship with Dorothy, he said, 'It was a turning point in his life. He gained a new confidence; he finally felt he could do something. And he got the opportunity to do so.'

I had met Dorothy Mierow in passing once or twice when I worked at ACAP: Chandra used to introduce her as his 'Aama'—his mother. The attachment was mutual. In an article that Dorothy wrote before her death in 2001, she called Chandra her son and heir: 'Among the Gurungs, women lacking children often adopt a son from a family that has several boys, as it is not considered good to be without a son.' She informally 'adopted' Chandra—taking on the ritual position of his dharma-mother. In 1973, Chandra moved into the house she lived in behind the museum. Chandra's younger sister Laxmi also lived with them. By then Dorothy was in her third term at the Peace Corps.

Upon finishing that term she returned to Colorado, taking Chandra with her. This proved to be the single most dramatic turn in Chandra's life: America. He enrolled at the Colorado

College and took classes for six months. Then, after hitchhiking across the United States, from friend to friend, acquaintance to acquaintance—a Nepali hippie footloose in that vast land—he eventually made his way to the United Kingdom. Having left Pokhara by then, his friend Michael Battye had just joined Reuters in London. Chandra stayed with his family in Yorkshire. Eventually he returned to Nepal, taking the hippie trail. More than a year had passed since he had left. He came back utterly changed.

'He had turned into a hippie,' said Birendrasingh. His hair was long, and his clothes were raggedy, scruffy. His sister Humkali's son in the Gurkhas, Major Hitman Gurung, recalled the shock: 'He had lice in his hair!' His soaltee Professor Jagman Gurung said, 'We all teased him, saying it must be very expensive to get a haircut in America.' But Chandra's world had expanded beyond all previous horizons.

'We had to talk sense into him,' Birendrasingh told me. They finally got him to cut his hair, but only before going to Siklis—out of consideration towards, or perhaps fear of, his father. Then Chandra went to Kathmandu to become a big person.

The natural history museum that Dorothy Mierow established still stands on the PN Campus grounds. I went there to see what I could find out about this woman who had so changed Chandra's life course. She was quite elderly by the time I met her, and I had not gained a sense of what lay beyond her schoolmarmish exterior.

In a campus of drab utilitarian structures, the museum stood out, cheery, with stone walls and a slate roof, and pillars carved in the shape of the 'people of Nepal'—men and women of a variety of ethnic groups wearing traditional clothes. The main exhibit hall inside boasted a concrete-and-enamel menagerie: plants and animals sculpted out of concrete, or painted on to the walls in a dense, tropical display. Stuffed and painted birds filled a smaller room beyond. Further on was a butterfly collection put together by a British naturalist, Colin Smith, whom I had also met while working at ACAP. (Thin, with a wispy white beard, he had had the flighty mannerisms of a butterfly himself.) School groups came daily to the museum, the children lingering over the butterfly exhibit: the blues and coppers, the swallowtails, the moths. I too spent a long while poring over the small, desiccated creatures, worrying over the fragility of their antennae, their powdery wings.

At the museum office I talked to Ramesh Shrestha of ACAP, who had worked with Dorothy after ACAP took charge of the museum—a move that Chandra had engineered in the 1990s to give continuity to both the museum and to Dorothy's position as its curator. Ramesh told me that Dorothy had made some of the museum displays herself. 'She was good at free-hand drawing, skilled at drawing birds and animals,' he said. It was Dorothy who had conceived of the rhinoceros and deer display in the main hall. Himself an artist, Ramesh spoke of technical matters: 'She preferred oils to acrylics. She particularly enjoyed colouring.' She had provided snacks for the museum staff while they worked on the displays, he said. Afterwards, when the work was done, she would host open-house parties.

But what had she been like as a person, I asked.

'She was tolerant. She was—different,' he said. He told me that she spoke fluent Nepali, and though secular, she had enjoyed Nepali festivals. But mostly she had focused on her work. Not only had she used her family's money to create the museum, she often bought art supplies out of her pocket, bringing paint sets back from the United States. Ramesh told me that Chandra had honoured the mother-son bond all her life. 'He never contradicted anything she said. Neither did she ever contradict him.'

I learned from others that Dorothy had just as strong a bond with Chandra's younger sister Laxmi. A childhood infection had ruptured Laxmi's eardrums; her hearing was poor. Dorothy took her to the United Kingdom in 1976, and put her in the charge of Michael Battye and John Welsh, former British volunteers. 'They persuaded the British socialized medicine authorities that Laxmi represented the Gurungs, who had been fighting as British Gurkhas, and thus she deserved this treatment,' Dorothy wrote in an article. Laxmi underwent five operations over the course of a year. Her hearing was eventually restored in one ear. When she returned to Nepal a year later, her English was also much improved. She, too, decided to study, to become a big person. Her chosen field was nursing.

'As a result of my "adoption" of Chandra and Laxmi,' Dorothy wrote, 'I have become a member of a Gurung family, and as the years have passed and my stays in Nepal have become more prolonged, my family has grown. I have become a mother and grandmother in the most painless and satisfying way possible.'

In her later years, Dorothy lived off campus, in Humkali's house. Family—a network that extended out from Siklis, all over the world, now including his American 'Aama' Dorothy—formed the foundation of Chandra's life. Despite his growing exposure to the world, he never rejected his roots. Instead, he built on that foundation. He treated Humkali's children, and all his nephews and nieces, as his own. They loved him back fiercely. In Pokhara, his nephew Krishnaman—who had once worked at ACAP—explained that he and his elder brother, Major Hitman Gurung, had grown up in Siklis under the care of Ratansingh and Krishnakumari during a difficult time in their parents' lives. 'We grew up as one family.' Chandra was always willing to help his family members study further, find work, prosper. But he was also a stern disciplinarian. 'He loved us, and also scolded us.' Though his uncle gave him a job at ACAP, he had to meet Chandra's very high standards. 'You couldn't get near him, he was so strict.'

It was the earnings of Humkali's eldest son, Major Hitman Gurung—who served in the Queen's Gurkha Signals in Dorset—that had built their family home in Pokhara. Not long before my visit to Pokhara, I met up with Major Hitman Gurung: I was in London for an overnight trip, and he was able to take a morning off to meet me at a coffee shop at Waterloo.

He was sharp and put-together, with a mix of warmth and confidence that immediately recalled Chandra. About his uncle, he echoed his younger brother's sentiments: 'He would do anything for the family.' Everyone in their family looked after each other, he said. That was why his parents had been able to make a success of all their nine children. (In addition to the major, one other brother was a Gurkha serviceman. Another was in the Singapore Police, and his other siblings had also studied, and prospered.)

Major Hitman Gurung mused over how proud Chandra was of his family; how proud he was, always, of his roots. He told me about how, when his parents came to visit him in the United Kingdom one year, Chandra insisted they wear traditional Gurung clothes. 'All my brothers and I, we told him—look, it's winter time, they'll be cold. But he insisted; he refused to listen. And—well, we couldn't say no to him.' So Ganga Bahadur and Humkali Gurung flew to the United Kingdom kitted in traditional Gurung dress. Upon arriving, of course, they quickly changed to more appropriate clothing. When Chandra found out about this, he scolded them. 'He said we should be proud of who we were,' Major Hitman Gurung said.

Chandra was, he said, particularly close to his mother, Humkali. 'He would say she had a gift, never showing how hard she had struggled, trying to turn us into what we are now.' In Pokhara I experienced her serene, steadfast affection for Chandra. She fed me, told me to stay at her house, opened her life to me. She said, 'You-all'—meaning those who had worked for Chandra at ACAP—'you must keep visiting us, even though he's gone. Stay here tonight. You-all remind me of him,' she said. She had a wide, pleasant face, the simple clothes of a village woman, and an unaffected manner. Though she was not lettered—she could not even write her own name, she said—Chandra had turned to her for advice. Whenever Chandra travelled abroad, he invariably called her a few days ahead to tell her he was going. He would call her again from the airport, just before departure. And he would call as soon as his plane landed back in Nepal.

Humkali's pride in Chandra was clear: 'When he was a child, the old grandfathers of the village would say—"this one, he'll become a big person,"' she told me. We were sitting at the back of her house on a grey, cloudy afternoon. She was crying as she spoke. She said, 'Later in life, our father would say—"he got all my brains, my know-how."' Even his early accomplishments had pleased his parents, she said. 'When he became a subba, our father had a buffalo killed, and he put on a feast for the whole village.' When Chandra visited Siklis, their father would go to the base of the village to meet him, taking along a contingent of villagers, and garlands, flowers, musicians. 'Father was so proud that he had a son like him, he would lavish money on the occasion. It was like the king was visiting.' She sighed. 'My younger brother was like a god to me. Sometimes,' she said, 'I think he's still here. I think—he's gone out for some work, he's just gone to the office for a little while, he'll be back.' She looked out at the clouds, pressing low in the heavy grey sky. It was the kind of weather in which she had lost her brother. 'When the weather is like this,' she said, 'I think of him.'

I took leave of her that afternoon, and returned to the Fewa Hotel, where I was staying. The clouds lowered over Pokhara in the evening, and it rained hard, the sky unburdening itself in sheets, walls of water blurring the horizon, joining the earth and sky. The rain kept up all night, and was still unrelenting in the morning. I sat on the hotel veranda, looking out. 'Tomorrow, if the weather is bad, don't go,' Humkali had told me when I left her house the previous afternoon. 'Come and stay here if your flight gets cancelled. You-all never need to stay in a hotel when you're here,' she had said. 'Just come here, stay here.'

As the morning wore on the rain kept coming; and the land absorbed it all, as though it were a sieve, or a bed of porous limestone. The downpour felt furious, biblical; I wondered if it was normal. Then I realized that the monsoon had broken.

There are six seasons in Nepal, each one lasting two months, and passing on. The currents off the Indian Ocean and the himals—or the barrier that they form—determine the pulls and pushes of the pressure systems, setting the seasons. In the preceding seasons of the year—basanta, springtime, and grishma, the hot, dry spell of mid April—the temperatures had risen on the Tibetan plateau, lowering the air pressure there. The resulting suction had drawn the moisture-laden air of the Indian Ocean northward through the transverse gorges in the himals and their foothills. Now, in barkha, the monsoon, this moisture had gathered in dense, rain-bearing clouds. The monsoon would end only in sharad, the autumn, in mid August. In hemanta, wintertime, in mid October, the air in the high mountains would cool again, becoming higher in pressure than the air on the Indian plateau (and the Indian Ocean). The suction would then draw the cold mountain air southward; and a northerly wind would blow in sishir, the cold, windy season, in mid December. This annual cycle would end after the maghe jhari, or the winter rains of mid February.

HE HYPNOTIZED PEOPLE

By the time Chandra returned from the United States and the United Kingdom by way of the hippie trail, he had honed his people skills, skills that would serve him all his life. He had the physical self-assurance of a young, strapping, good-looking man. But he was also endowed with an unusual personal magnetism. Everyone I talked to about him mentioned this, using different terms. Judith Amtzis, who taught him in a preparation class for the Test of English as a Foreign Language, remembered him, thirty years on, as being very charismatic, always drawing the class together as a group of friends. 'Maybe because he was so tall,' suggested Dibya Gurung, a colleague of mine at ACAP, 'he was very confident.' Others suggested that being the son of a mukhiya had given him a strong sense of self. He had a quality, a gift, of charming others effortlessly. 'He hypnotized people,' his nephew Major Hitman Gurung told me in London: 'He cast a kind of spell. Even people who had met him only once felt close to him.' Almost everyone recalled that he never patronized, never condescended. Pitambar Sharma, who taught him at Tribhuvan University, said, 'Maybe because he had risen from the bottom, he genuinely cared about the "small" people.' Neither did he fail to respect 'big' people. 'He knew how to fulfil all the formalities,' was how his cousin Badri Gurung put it. 'He knew how to make things just right.' 'He was gifted at public relations,' said his soaltee Professor Jagman Gurung. Siddhartha Bajra Bajracharya, who had worked for Chandra at ACAP, used the same words: 'He had excellent PR.' Shailendra Thakali, another ACAP colleague, laughed about the effect he had on donors in particular: 'He had only to open his mouth, and they'd offer money. All he had to do was ask, and they'd give him anything he wanted.'

Many others alluded to his appeal to women. From college on there had never been a shortage of women around Chandra, and he had acquired a reputation as a 'boy who plays with girls', as the Nepali expression goes. That he liked women was obvious. What was harder to know was how many of his relations were friendships, flirtations or more serious involvements.

At Tribhuvan University, Sumitra Manandhar fell under Chandra's spell. 'He had come back from abroad, and he seemed—different,' she said when we talked about their marriage at his house in Dhapasi, Kathmandu. Long estranged from Chandra, she had been to this house only upon Chandra's death, to host the funeral rites. The house was elegant, with airy, modern spaces and traditional Gurung and Newar design elements. It was a house that Chandra had designed with his second wife, Tokiko Sato. Sumitra and I sat in Chandra's study, lined with bookshelves and a raadi, a thick handwoven wool rug with a hatched motif, from the Annapurna area.

Sumitra was twenty-two years old when she and Chandra were graduate students at the Tribhuvan University's geography department. This was in 1976. He was twenty-seven. According to Pitambar Sharma, who taught them both, she was by far the better student. She went on to establish herself as a consultant and civil rights activist, acquiring the robust confidence of someone just as comfortable in the remotest villages as in the glitziest seminars. She earned a place for herself in Kathmandu society. But as a young woman in the 1970s, she defied all family expectation by delaying marriage just to pursue a master's degree. Then, on top of that, to be romantically involved with a man—a Gurung man from an unheard-of village called Siklis, no less—amounted to an all-out rebellion.

I tried to draw her out on the whens and hows of their romance, but she would not divulge these. 'He was good at making friends,' was what she said. Chandra was an intriguing blend of traditional and bohemian, village and international. She, too, would have been a novelty to him: a modern Nepali woman intent on leading a professional life. By their second year of studies they were romantically involved.

Their courtship seemed to have been a heady, intellectual one. As part of its mission of nation-building—development—the Panchayat regime had just launched the 'Gaun Farka Abhiyan', or the Return to the Village Campaign, to strengthen urban-rural linkages. Chandra and Sumitra were in the first batch of university students required to spend ten months in the countryside, in a programme known as the National Development Service. (The programme ended not many years later, in part for forcing reluctant urban students out of their comfortable milieus, and in part for radicalizing them by exposing them to the poverty of the countryside.)

Students were assigned to different parts of the country based on a lottery. Chandra's lottery dispatched him to the districts of Gulmi and Surkhet, in the far-western hills. Sumitra went to the districts of Kaski and Lamjung—key Gurung areas. Over this separation they corresponded by post, and during the Dashain holidays Chandra came to visit Sumitra. They went together to Pokhara, staying at Dorothy Mierow's house. Shortly after that, during the Tihar festival, Sumitra came to Kathmandu and told her parents that she and Chandra were going to get married.

The Manandhars are a caste of the Newars, the indigenous people of the Kathmandu valley. Originally oil pressers, they are also known by their original name, Sayami. Like so many ethnic/indigenous nationalities, they are proud of who they are, and prickly about their status. Sumitra's family were well-established traders, the first to import bicycles to Kathmandu. For the traditionalists among them, like Sumitra's father, a Gurung man from Siklis—even if he was the son of a mukhiya, and a Gothane Gurung, of a 'high' four-jaat Tamu clan—would have been utterly undesirable as a son-in-law. Sumitra's father came down firmly against the match.

Nor were Ratansingh and Krishnakumari overjoyed when Chandra told them he had found a modern Kathmandu woman, a Newar. As Professor Jagman Gurung told me, 'Of course they didn't come out and say it, but they would have liked him to settle down with a Gurung-seni,' a Gurung woman. But it was Sumitra whom Chandra had chosen; and his parents deferred to him. The rest of the family, too, accepted the choice. His brother Totraman was working in Kathmandu as a community health trainer for the Peace Corps at the time. His sister Laxmi was also in Kathmandu, studying nursing. They all rented an apartment together in the neighbourhood of Baluwatar. Sumitra got to know them all well.

It reveals how small Nepal's academic circles were at the time that Pitambar Sharma, who taught Chandra at Tribhuvan University, had himself been taught there by Harka Gurung. (The three remained close all throughout.) Upon graduating from Tribhuvan University, Chandra went to Bangkok for further studies at the Asian Institute of Technology. Pitambar Sharma told me about this period in Chandra's life. Professor Sharma's wife, who worked as a flight attendant—an air hostess—helped book Chandra's plane ticket. 'I'd hear about his progress from mutual friends,' he told me. 'Chandra found a place to live at AIT's Asia Centre, and earned a bit of money by giving lectures. He was quick that way.' He laughed. 'He picked up a bit of Thai, to make local friends. He joined the student union, and even served as the secretary.'

Chandra's area of study at AIT concerned 'people's participation'—the imperative to grant the people of any given area a say in government (and non-government) development schemes. Most development work tended to have a centralized, top-down, paternalistic approach. An attempt to reverse this, and to put local people in charge of their own area's development, the philosophy of 'people's participation', would shape all of Chandra's future work.

Sumitra, at the time, worked in Kathmandu for the United Nations on what she described to me as a 'highland and lowland interactive system'. (The development world is replete with such jargon.) It was during this period that Chandra's younger sister Laxmi, still studying nursing, developed a persistent cough. Laxmi had always had trouble gaining weight. The family—close as they were—consulted each other about this. From Bangkok, Chandra insisted that she see a doctor. Their brother Totraman's links through the Peace Corps proved useful. A US embassy doctor examined Laxmi, and found that she had tuberculosis. She was immediately hospitalized at the Mission Hospital.

Sumitra was with the family when Laxmi was discharged from the hospital two weeks later. Back home, Laxmi went into the bathroom to take a shower. 'She vomited blood, and fell,' Sumitra told me. She was found unconscious by her cousin Badri Gurung. Laxmi never revived. She was twenty-three years old. Sumitra told me that the entire family was devastated: 'I think they felt they should have prevented it, they never forgave themselves for it, somehow.' Chandra, too, was devastated, she said. I heard as much from his friend and physician, Dr Buddha Basnet. Decades later, recounting his sister's death to Dr Basnet, tears sprang to Chandra's eyes.

Laxmi's death delayed the wedding plans of Chandra and Sumitra, but their relationship remained on course. Returning to Nepal during the summer holidays, Chandra took Sumitra to Siklis, where she met Ratansingh and Krishnakumari and other relatives. As Jagman Gurung told me, this was a significant sign of her acceptance into the family. 'The family received her, even in the village,' he said. 'Both his father and mother accepted her publicly.'

Sumitra's father was still opposed to the match, though. The following year—1981—Sumitra enrolled at AIT, defiantly telling her family, before leaving Kathmandu, that she and Chandra were going to get married in Bangkok. Chandra was already in his last few months of study when she got to Bangkok. He was working as a research assistant. They settled into a life together. Chandra's cousin Badri Gurung visited them on a business trip. 'They lived together, even though they weren't married,' he told me. Chandra was as sociable as ever. 'He would put on Nepali clothes, and create shows, whether or not he knew what he was doing,' Badri said. Photographs of him at the time show him at the peak of youthfulness, attractiveness. He was constantly surrounded by friends, both Nepali and international. Many of them were women.

Chandra's mishandling of his marriages—first to Sumitra, then to Tokiko—became one of his enduring failures, a source of heartache for him and also, to differing degrees, for his two wives and four children. He and Sumitra got engaged at AIT, with a Catholic oath and a Buddhist chant of refuge. A month later they got married with little ceremony, registering at a district office. The best man at the wedding was Ramesh Manandhar, a relative of Sumitra and a close friend of Chandra who died in a Thai Airways crash in Kathmandu in 1992. A few other friends came along as witnesses. The signing of the marriage certificate was followed with shagun, a Newari ritual feast, among friends.

Chandra left AIT within three months of Sumitra's arrival in Bangkok. For her—now Sumitra Manandhar Gurung—this separation proved more difficult than any of their previous periods apart. She and Chandra were married now; and yet there remained, she said, much uncertainty about their life together. Moving into a dormitory after Chandra's departure, she became completely distraught.

Chandra, for his part, was determined to continue higher studies. Before leaving Bangkok he had applied to the University of Hawaii to pursue a PhD. His area of specialization was to be medical geography. He needed, now, to conduct field-based research on morbidity factors. In Kathmandu, he reconnected with Pitambar Sharma, who was then working as the chief adviser at the Population Commission. Professor Sharma knew that the USAID funded work on migration. He was able to arrange funds for Chandra's study.

The study completed, Chandra headed to the University of Hawaii's East-West Center in Honolulu to begin the course work for his PhD. This was where his marriage to Sumitra began to unravel for good, as he fell in love with Tokiko Sato, a graduate student at the University of Hawaii who was also pursuing a PhD.

At Bangkok AIT, Sumitra rushed through her courses, completing them within fifteen months, and skipping the graduation ceremony in order to return to start her PhD in Hawaii. Following in Chandra's footsteps, she had applied to the University of Hawaii. She flew to Honolulu to join her husband.

He came to the airport to receive her, she told me, in Tokiko Sato's car, telling her that it belonged to a friend. He was supporting himself as a teaching assistant at the East-West Center. Sumitra too found work as a teaching assistant. They lived in cramped quarters, with the usual tribulations of cash-strapped students. Sumitra found her husband 'changed', she told me. He would argue with her about the smallest things. 'He even got angry about cooking,' she said.

She did not know the reason for his anger; and in this she was alone. 'Everyone except for Sumitra knew about the other relationship,' Pitambar Sharma recalled. He reached the East-West Center as a fellow just as Chandra was finishing up there. 'Or maybe she did know, but didn't take it seriously. Maybe she thought it was just a fling, and that their marriage would eventually improve,' he said.

When Sumitra did discover Chandra's relationship with Tokiko Sato, she happened to be suffering from salmonella poisoning. The discovery threw her into crisis. She lost weight, going down to a drastic seventy-seven pounds. She told Chandra she wanted to go back to Nepal, but—for reasons one can only guess at—he encouraged her to stay on, assuring her that his relationship with Tokiko was over.

As Sumitra said to me, 'He shouldn't have lied.'

'He was like a child,' commented his soaltee Jagman Gurung. Chandra was unable, it seemed, to make either woman unhappy. Or perhaps he loved them both. He did genuinely respect Sumitra: on the rare occasions that he talked about her to ACAP staff he had nothing but praise for her, exhorting the women staff to become like her. Or perhaps he was too weak to end his marriage so early. Guilt may also have played a part, for he knew that she had defied her family to marry him, a boy from Siklis. Maybe he could not quite face up to the magnitude of his betrayal of her.

Sumitra told me that they did try to repair their marriage. But when her sister visited them in Honolulu a year later, she found them both intensely unhappy. They had moved into more spacious married students' housing by then, but their bickering had not ceased. At one point, Sumitra went to

Kathmandu to attend a seminar and Chandra stayed back to take his comprehensive exams. While in Kathmandu she learned that he had failed. They studied for the exam together after she returned to Honolulu. What Sumitra did not know—till much later—was that during her absence, Tokiko Sato had given birth to a son, Yoichi: her and Chandra's firstborn.

In the months after Chandra's death I tried to contact Tokiko Sato about their relationship and eventual marriage, but she—in the throes of grief—was reluctant, and I did not feel it my business to press her. Those who have met her have said she is dignified, and strong. Upon completing her PhD at the University of Hawaii she went to work in international aid in Nairobi and Jordan. To me, she offered this much about Chandra, by email: 'He was a very good man to us as a father and a husband. Maybe he was most relaxed when he was with us as well as when he was with his sister's family. We miss him a lot.'

The confusion Chandra experienced—and caused—in his family life did not affect him professionally. He wanted to return to Nepal to work. Many other Nepali students he had studied with in Bangkok and in Hawaii had taken international jobs. Chandra never pursued this option. In 1984, both he and Sumitra came to Nepal to research their theses. Her research centred on the village of Kakani, on the outskirts of Kathmandu, while his centred on Siklis.

During this period the couple tried again to repair their marriage. Sumitra's family belatedly recognized their union, formally welcoming Chandra into their home with a Newari ceremony. They lived together in Kathmandu, and it was then that Sumitra became pregnant. Their daughter, Amanda, was born at the Mission Hospital in 1985.

'The rituals were all opposite,' Sumitra said of the Newari and Gurung customs for welcoming a child into the world. By Newari custom, mother and child are sequestered for fear of contamination. Gurung tradition is to greet childbirth with public celebration. Such differences gave rise to misgivings in both families. Both, after all, were proud; both were well established in their own places. When interacting with each other, they seemed to feel slighted in small but needling ways. In particular, Chandra felt that Sumitra's family—Kathmandu urbanites—looked down on his as villagers, as hicks.

When, after completing their research, the couple returned to Hawaii to write their theses, Chandra once again went back to Tokiko Sato. He was obviously very drawn to her, as he kept discovering in a muddle. He and Sumitra had brought Amanda to Honolulu. One of Chandra's nieces had also come to help care for the baby. A bitter feud developed, however, between Sumitra and Chandra's niece: Sumitra felt the niece was encouraging Chandra's relationship with Tokiko. What Sumitra did not know was that Chandra and Tokiko had a son to bind them.

Chandra now had nothing but impatience for his wife. They occupied separate rooms in the apartment they shared in the university's married students' housing complex. Newar/Gurung tensions flared up between them, for Amanda was being raised to speak Newari as her mother tongue. Chandra felt left out by this. Husband and wife were barely on speaking terms eventually. As the academic pressure mounted, they decided to send Amanda back to Nepal, to be raised awhile by Sumitra's family. Chandra's niece also returned to Nepal, undoubtedly in great relief.

Then, one day, Chandra handed Sumitra a letter in which he demanded a divorce. To Sumitra, this was unthinkable. She did not agree to a divorce then, or ever. One of their Nepali friends in Honolulu talked Chandra into reconsidering. During a brief reconciliation, Sumitra again became pregnant with their son, Adhish.

No one can know, of course, what was going on in Chandra's mind through all this passion, turbulence, love and heartbreak. In 1988, he returned to Nepal for good, a PhD: Dr Chandraprasad Gurung. Sumitra stayed behind for a few months to defend her thesis. In Kathmandu, Chandra spent some weeks at his in-laws with his daughter. Then he went to Siklis to pay his parents a visit. By the time Sumitra returned to Nepal—five months pregnant—Chandra was living in the village of Ghandruk, in the Annapurna area, working for the King Mahendra Trust for Nature Conservation.

ROYAL PATRONAGE

Talking to me, Sumitra Manandhar Gurung had been very open about her marriage with Chandra. She had also been generous about him. At one point, she said something that resonated with me long afterwards. We had talked about his abandoning her after their return from Hawaii, his long absences from their children during their early years, and the heated legal negotiations they had gone through to reach a childcare agreement. Though Sumitra had criticized Chandra for these failings, she had praised what he went on to do professionally. 'He couldn't give that much to us, but he gave everything he had to the community,' she had said, thoughtfully. 'What he couldn't do for his family, he did for others, you see.'

By 'the community', she had meant his own people, the people of the Annapurna area—the Gurung people—but she also meant the people of Nepal. Chandra gave to the community through his work in conservation, a field that he happened into by chance, by circumstance, rather than by design. His expertise, after all, was in medical geography; his interest lay in development. He had no knowledge of the natural sciences. It was the pioneering environmentalist Hemanta Mishra who—upon hiring him at the King Mahendra Trust for Nature Conservation—inducted him into conservation. It was the trust that turned Chandra into an environmentalist.

Conservation was then a wide-open field in Nepal. What efforts had taken place had focused on saving one or another species—the rhinoceros, the tiger—in the plains south of the Churia range, in the tarai. Before 1950, this area was a dense jungle. The sparse inhabitants trod lightly on the land. The main human threat to the wildlife then came from the annual hunts, or shikar, of the ruling Shah and Rana dynasties. Shikar was a long-established tradition of the maharajas of the princely Mughal states before and after British rule. Nepal's Shah kings adopted the practice after the country's unification by Prithvi Narayan Shah in 1768. Shikar had become a part of court life by 1849, when the Rana maharajas began their rule.

The Rana-era hunts were grand, requiring the mobilization of the entire court. Tulsi Ram Vaidya, Triratna Manandhar and Shankar Lal Joshi have written, in *Social History of Nepal*, that for a single expedition Jung Bahadur Kunwar Rana took hundreds of officials with him to the tarai, along with '32,000 soldiers, 52 guns, 300 horsemen, 250 horse artillery, 2000 followers and 700 rations officers'. Hoping to curry favour, subsequent Rana maharajas began to invite the maharajas and colonial officials of British India along. These invitations were coveted by the invitees, for game was more plentiful in the Nepal tarai than in most of the other hunting grounds of northern India.

In 1911, Maharaja Chandra Sumshere Jung Bahadur Rana invited King George V to Chitwan, in the tarai, for a hunt in which, according to a 1912 report in *The New York Times*, the king personally killed thirty-seven tigers, nineteen rhinoceroses, and countless lesser game. 'Cars Ran into Tigers', declared *The New York Times*'s breathless headline. The story detailed the luxury at the camp, where electricity was installed temporarily, and where a European-style breakfast was served each morning: 'Porridge. Bekti Maitre d'Hotel. Oeufs aux choux saucisses. Grillies. Curry de legumes viandes. Froides. Café.'

The next shikar to involve the British royal family took place in 1921, when the Prince of Wales killed seventeen tigers, ten rhinoceroses, two leopards and two bears. Another particularly resplendent shikar took place in 1939, when Maharaja Juddha Sumshere Jung Bahadur Rana invited the British viceroy—Victor Alexander John Hope, Marquess of Linlithgow—to the Chitwan. The viceroy killed 120 tigers, thirty-eight rhinoceroses, twenty-seven leopards and fifteen sloth bears during that hunt.

According to Nina Bhatt's article 'Kings as Wardens and Wardens as Kings', the Rana maharajas also encouraged the Shah kings, who were under their control, to hunt—as a means of diverting them, and distracting them from trying to regain power. Thus the living rooms of many a Shah and Rana home in Kathmandu today still boast many moth-eaten hunting trophies.

All this took a toll on the wildlife of the tarai. According to Hemanta Mishra in his memoir, *The Soul of the Rhino*, only two hundred years ago, the greater Asian one-horned rhinoceros, *Rhinoceros unicornis*, inhabited a vast area in South Asia, from the Indus River in present-day Pakistan in the west to Burma and the southern reaches of China in the east.

Today they survive only in India and in Nepal's tarai, that too in small, fragmented communities. At the turn of the twentieth century, by the account of WWF Nepal, the rhinoceros population in the jungles of Chitwan was approximately 1,000. The rhinoceros has no predator in the animal world; humans are its sole threat. By the mid 1960s, Chitwan's rhinoceros population had shrunk to a startling ninety.

Like the rhinoceros, the tiger is considered by environmentalists to be a 'flagship' animal, an animal whose abundance or scarcity mirrors the health of its habitat. Of the eight original tiger subspecies worldwide, the Caspian, Javan and Bali subspecies have become extinct due to unregulated hunting and habitat loss. The remaining five species—the Royal Bengal, the Siberian, the Sumatran, the Indochinese and the South China—are all endangered now, critically so, with a combined worldwide population of only 5,000. (At the turn of the twentieth century, the tiger population was 100,000 worldwide.) The only tiger found in the tarai is the Royal Bengal: *Panthera tigris tigris*. According to WWF Nepal, the Royal Bengal tiger was already endangered by 1940. Most of the 3,176 to 4,556 that are now living are found in India. Approximately 123 live in the tarai today.

The other endangered animals of the tarai include the wild Asian elephant, the swamp deer, the hispid hare, the sloth bear, the wild water buffalo, the black buck, and the four-horned antelope. Their habitat came under accelerated destruction after 1950, when Nepal launched on its mission to develop. In particular, the eradication of malaria—following a global campaign by the World Health Organization—helped to make the tarai more habitable for people. When King

Mahendra Bir Bikram Shah took absolute power in 1960, he instituted a policy of mass migration—relocating the people of the hills to the tarai, which was more cultivable, and agriculturally more productive than the hills.

By then the Forest Nationalization Act of 1957 had taken ownership of the forests away from those who lived in them and invested full ownership in the state. This enabled mass clearing of the forests for human settlement. The depleted settlements of today's tarai are stark illustration, perhaps, of the position of human beings as the earth's most dominant animals. This is a species still multiplying worldwide. Ten thousand years ago there were ten million people on earth. Today we number more than 6.6 billion, and that number is set to rise to nine billion by 2050. Half of Nepal's population came to live in the tarai. The local ecology was irrevocably changed as agriculture altered and simplified the composition of the local flora, and as grazing led to further depletion. Poaching also posed a new threat, with a burgeoning national and international market for rare pelts and animal parts. By the 1970s, vast swathes of the tarai forests had been lost. What remained of the wilderness was broken into ecological 'islands': small, unviable areas surrounded by human habitation.

Yet, if the development of Nepal after 1950 made the country vulnerable to environmental destruction, it also opened it to new ideas, including ideas about the environmental movement, which in the West was newly galvanized by Rachel Carson's 1962 publication of *Silent Spring*, on the unforeseen damages wrought by DDT.

As in much of the rest of the world, conservation in Nepal

began as an attempt by well-placed hunters to protect their gaming lands from further human encroachment. The hunters in this case were members of Nepal's royal family. The Shah kings took up the cause not out of their own initiative, but out of the initiative of the country's pioneering environmentalists.

One of these pioneers was Hemanta Mishra. He writes, in *The Soul of the Rhino*, of a rhinoceros census that he worked on in 1968, assisting an environmentalist from New Zealand, Graeme Caughley. Funded by the United Nations, the census concluded that not only was the rhinoceros population down to between ninety and 108, but the rhinoceros would be locally extinct by the late 1980s if the trends of the day continued. A Kathmanduite with family links to the royal court, Hemanta Mishra was aware of King Mahendra's love of hunting.

Indeed, King Mahendra and his brothers, Prince Himalaya and Prince Basundhara, conducted shikar all over the tarai, from east to west. (They also crossed the border to hunt: at the bird sanctuary in the Keoladeo National Park in Bharatpur, India, is a placard recording the 3 April 1957 hunt of the King of Nepal: 76 bags with 26 guns, over a half-day shoot.) As the Rana maharajas had, the Shah kings too invited foreign dignitaries to Nepal to hunt. In 1961, soon after taking absolute power, King Mahendra hosted a tiger hunt during Queen Elizabeth and Prince Philip's state visit to Nepal. The hunt took place in Meghauli. The airport built for it still operates today. To make the hunt more efficient—for the state visit was brief—a tiger was corralled beforehand into a pen. One can only speculate on what the UK royals thought of this; for by then Prince Philip was already a champion of conservation, and even the former maharajas of India had begun to frown on the hunting of tigers. The ethics of hunting would itself disapprove of shooting a corralled animal. In this case, the guests were on elephant back, sipping refreshments. Offered a chance to shoot the tiger, Queen Elizabeth modestly declined. Prince Philip too cited a boil on his trigger finger. It fell to Prince Philip's treasurer, Rear Admiral Christopher Bonham Carter, and Queen Elizabeth's secretary, Sir Michael Adeane, to shoot the tiger, which they did, inelegantly, after several failed attempts. A 1961 *Time* magazine report on the hunt was titled 'Hapless Hunting'.

While working on the rhinoceros census in 1968, Hemanta Mishra saw an opportunity in the royal penchant for shikar. 'A copy of our report was discreetly passed directly to King Mahendra, through the help of my father's friends,' Mishra writes in *The Soul of a Rhino*. 'Alerting this wildlife-loving Nepalese king was the only way of getting quick action in the slow-moving bureaucracy of Nepal.'

His strategy proved effective. King Mahendra famously died of a heart attack during a 1972 shikar in Chitwan. By then he had ordered the drafting of conservation legislation.

The next king, Birendra Bir Bikram Shah, was not as avid a hunter, but he and his family—including his brothers Gyanendra Shah and Dhirendra Shah—continued the tradition of shikar. They were not skilled marksmen: Hemanta Mishra writes that during one shikar, Prince Dhirendra accidentally shot his stepmother, Queen Mother Ratna. By this time the maharajas of India had turned into serious environmentalists: Project Tiger was launched in India in 1973. In Nepal, too, environmentalists tried to educate the royal family.

They did and did not succeed. In 1972, following through on a decree by his father, King Birendra ordered the establishment of Nepal's first national park, the Royal Chitwan National Park. To establish it, 22,000 local people were evicted. Tirtha Man Maskey was appointed the park's first warden. In 1973, the government passed the National Parks and Wildlife Conservation Act. The Royal Chitwan National Park was protected, at the start, by a gainda gasti, a 'rhinoceros patrol'. It later came under the guard of the Royal Nepal Army.

Despite this gesture towards conservation, the tradition of royal shikar remained in place through the Panchayat era, and even after the restoration of democracy in 1990. The hunts put on by the Shah kings were not much different from those put on by the Rana maharajas. Tirtha Man Maskey's widow, Laxmibadan Maskey has written of them in *Tiger Warden*, a memoir of her life with her husband. The national park staff had to assist full-time when a royal hunt was on, she has written. Preparations for these hunts got under way months before the royal family arrived. After flying in on helicopters, royal family members would settle into the best local accommodations. Their hunting day started at 6 a.m. All but the 'queens'—Queen Aishwarya and her sisters Princesses Komal and Prekchya, who were married to Prince Gyanendra and Prince Dhirendra—went on the hunts. The queens played cards, usually a game called marriage. Her husband's duties ended only when the royal family left. 'When the kings were there, there was no chance of his having any free time,' Laxmibadan Maskey writes. 'Only when the kings all went back did he have any time to himself. Not even free time: just the feeling that a big hassle had come to an end.'

The hunting committee of the royal palace directed the hunts. But as Nina Bhatt has pointed out, it is difficult to know what, if any, regulations the committee put in place. Tigers and rhinoceroses—classified as endangered—were by now officially off-limits, thanks to pressure created by environmentalists. Quotas were set for other animals; but Prince Gyanendra sat in on the meetings that set the quotas, and no one dared to openly disagree with him. Writes Nina Bhatt: 'Indeed, these were valuable opportunities for park staff to ingratiate favors with the palace by insisting on a generous quota.'

Laxmibadan Maskey writes, 'When the king [and his family came], they mostly hunted rhinoceroses, tigers, deer, antelopes, bears and alligators.' If they were going to hunt tigers, the beasts would be encircled a full day ahead, to make things easier for the hunters. 'Tigers are never hunted without encircling them.' In her innocence she adds: 'I think that might be a rule. They search out a place where there are tigers, and encircle them. I think rhinoceroses are found more easily. And you don't have to search that hard for deer and antelopes.'

None of this was, strictly, illegal, since members of the royal family were above the law during the Panchayat era. Even after 1990 they enjoyed impunity. But it did engender resentment locally. The people living near the national park came to view the park staff as guarding the jungles for the exclusive use of the royal family. It did not help that some of the army personnel guarding the parks indulged in hunting, and even poaching and the smuggling of wildlife contraband. The Royal Nepal Army, for its part, behaved as though the people of the area were menaces to be kept away by the use of force. This led to parks-vs-people conflicts and, more generally, to an erosion of trust regarding the entire concept of conservation.

In hindsight—looking back from a Nepal that has abolished the monarchy—it is easy to see the perils of seeking royal patronage for conservation. Yet Nepal's pioneering environmentalists clearly found this the most expedient way of pushing through conservation policy.

In 1974, the young King Birendra asked his brother Prince Gyanendra to establish a network of national parks and wildlife reserves throughout the country. This turned Prince Gyanendra into the main patron of conservation in Nepal. Over the years royal patronage enabled the establishment of the Royal Shuklaphanta Wildlife Reserve (declared a hunting reserve in 1969, and gazetted as a wildlife reserve in 1973), the Sagarmatha National Park (1976), the Langtang National Park (declared in 1972, and gazetted in 1976), the Koshi Tappu Wildlife Reserve (1976), the Rara National Park (1976), the Shey Phoksundo National Park (1984), the Parsa Wildlife Reserve (1984), the Khaptad National Park (1985), the Shivapuri National Park (1985), the Royal Bardiya National Park (1988) and the Makalu-Barun National Park and Conservation Area (1991). (As with the Chitwan National Park, the parks in Shuklaphanta and Bardiya are no longer called 'Royal'.) The Dhorpatan Hunting Reserve was established in 1987. Three further conservation areas were established in the 1990s—in the Annapurna area, the Manasalu area and in Kangchanjunga. Almost 20 per cent of Nepal's total landmass now falls under one or another kind of protection, in what today's environmentalists consider a major achievement.

By the time Prince Gyanendra came to be the main patron of conservation in Nepal, he had gained a reputation for misusing his royal privileges for private gain. Worse, he was said to have links to the underworld of drug and idol smuggling, of organized crime. In the Panchayat era—an era of simmering political discontent and suppressed democratic aspirations—it was also easy for those who opposed the absolute monarchy to spread rumours of the prince's involvement in wildlife poaching, and in the smuggling of wildlife contraband.

Nevertheless, Hemanta Mishra—who was largely responsible for turning the prince into an environmentalist—remains unambiguous in his praise:

> Through his personal contacts and royal connections, the prince had been instrumental in forging Nepal's relationship with the Smithsonian Institution, the World Wildlife Fund, and the World Conservation Union. Though he was not popular in many Nepali political circles, I found him to be a kindhearted intellectual with a deep commitment to nature conservation.

But it did not help that the royal family kept up the tradition of shikar, enlisting the national park staff as aids. So unreformed was the royal family that even environmentalists suffered direct conflicts of interest. Hemanta Mishra's memoir, *The Soul of the Rhino*, culminates in his receiving a confidential letter from the royal palace in 1978, ordering him to organize a rhinoceros hunt for King Birendra. This, for a ritual called the tarpan, which Hemanta Mishra learned, to his dismay, the Shah kings felt duty-bound to perform at least once upon ascending to the throne. The tarpan was said to date back to the Rajput maharajas of India in the ninth and tenth centuries. It required a new king to sacrifice the blood of a male rhinoceros to his ancestors, and even to enter its disembowelled carcass as part of the ritual.

'The order hit me hard,' writes Hemanta Mishra:

> I was a Western-educated scientist and did not believe in these superstitious ceremonies. Furthermore, I was a member of the Species Survival Commission of the International Union for the Conservation of Nature and Natural Resources (World Conservation Union)—a Swiss-based global custodian of flora and fauna. Rhinos topped the list of rare and endangered species in the Union's Red Data Book.

The hunt threatened to invite infamy, scandal. But his objections were easily overridden, and not just by the court. 'Surprisingly,' he notes, 'some of the supporters of the rhino hunt were not even Nepalese but a few Western anthropologists who had flocked to Nepal in the seventies. They openly voiced concerns that young, Western-educated youths like me did not know the significance of our own cultural practices.'

Prince Gyanendra himself presided over the meeting of the

royal palace hunting committee to decide whether or not to go ahead with the tarpan. To no one's surprise, the meeting decided in favour of the rhinoceros hunt. All Hemanta Mishra managed to do—to ward off scandal—was to persuade the committee to broadcast news of it publicly, and to explain its cultural significance: the hunting of a rhinoceros by a king was not akin to the hunting by a common poacher. On Prince Gyanendra's orders he also informed the World Conservation Union, the World Wildlife Fund, the National Geographic Society and the Smithsonian Institution about the hunt.

The next few chapters of *The Soul of the Rhino* detail the hunt, just outside the Royal Chitwan National Park, till—'"Bang!" went the monarch's rifle.' A description of the gruesome, atavistic ritual follows. The king had to enter the carcass of the disembowelled rhinoceros to perform his ancestor worship. By the end, however, even Hemanta Mishra had been won over: 'Killing one rhino was both a cultural and a political necessity,' he writes. 'Moreover, as aptly pointed out by an anthropologist, the Tarpan elevated the rhino to a royal or sacred status. And in many ways this helped preserve the species.'

From today's perspective it seems obvious that just as the environmentalists used the royal family to push through conservation policy, the royal family used the environmentalists to do as they pleased. 'Anyway, what choice do you have?' Hemanta Mishra's wife asked him at one point, as he was agonizing over the ethics of the rhinoceros hunt. Of course everyone has a choice. Hemanta Mishra chose to work for conservation from within the Panchayat system. This was the choice that all of Nepal's pioneering environmentalists made: to make the most of an imperfect situation.

The payback, in terms of conservation, was not inconsiderable. In 1982, King Birendra decreed the establishment of the King Mahendra Trust for Nature Conservation. A non-government organization, the trust nevertheless enjoyed quasi-government status as the king himself was its patron, and Prince Gyanendra was the chairman of the board. During the Panchayat era, all non-government organizations were regulated by the Social Services National Coordinating Committee, headed by Queen Aishwarya. (The 'coordination' done by this body usually amounted to controlling all funds.) By directly involving the king and the prince, the trust was able to bypass this body. Hemanta Mishra was appointed its director, as the member-secretary.

THE ACCIDENTAL ENVIRONMENTALIST

This was what the field of conservation was like when Hemanta Mishra hired Chandra at the trust. Chandra started off as a consultant. Mingma Norbu Sherpa was also working there as a consultant. Even more so than Chandra, Mingma was a self-made man. He too was born in a village. The son of a high-altitude porter who died in a mountaineering expedition, Mingma had studied at a school that Edmund Hillary had opened in the village of Khumjung, at the base of Mt Everest. With the help of Edmund Hillary's charitable foundation, he had gone on to study at the Lincoln College in New Zealand and the University of Manitoba in Canada. He held a master's degree in natural resources management, and was working as a warden at the Sagarmatha National Park—the first Sherpa ever to hold that post—when Hemanta Mishra, who had helped to establish that national park in consultation with Edmund Hillary, had him deputed to the trust.

Everyone who witnessed the long partnership between Mingma and Chandra acknowledges that Mingma was the more focused environmentalist. Chandra, though, suffused their work with spirit. 'Mingma was the head, and Chandra was the heart,' was how WWF's Ghana Shyam Gurung (Ghurmet) described their partnership, which lasted for the rest of their lives.

Tirtha Man Maskey was slowly moving up the government ranks at the time. Together, Hemanta Mishra, Tirtha Man Maskey, Mingma Norbu Sherpa, Chandra and other environmentalists began mulling over the need for more, and more effective, protected areas in Nepal. They particularly wanted to avoid the parks-vs-people conflict that had occurred in the Royal Chitwan National Park. Throughout the world, the concept of 'protected areas' was cropping up as an alternative to national parks. Unlike in national parks, protected areas did not require the displacement of people: they included human settlements within their bounds.

There was also a serious drive, at the time, to revise all of Nepal's forest management policies. These had remained unchanged for many decades following the establishment of the Department of Forests in 1942. In 1978, with a growing concern about deforestation, the government passed a law requiring the panchayats, the local government, to protect the forests in their areas. Yet, because this law offered no incentive to the local people, it ultimately proved less than effective.

At the time, Australian Aid was pursuing community forestry in the district of Kavre. Community forestry, which had proven effective in Australia, granted local communities (rather than the government) responsibility for managing local forests. The United Kingdom, Finland and Denmark were keen on promoting community forestry in Nepal. Among the Nepali experts supporting community forestry were Dr Tej B. S. Mahat, the dean of the Institute of Forestry in Pokhara, and Amrit Lal Joshi, the planning chief of the Ministry of Forests and Soil Conservation. Though no one explicitly framed it as such, community forestry was an inherently democratic exercise. It was also part of a growing call for the decentralization of power.

In 1989, a twenty-five-year Master Plan for the Forestry Sector formally recognized that the forests should primarily benefit the communities, rather than the government. It decreed that all accessible hill forests be handed over to 'community forest user groups', insofar as these groups were capable of managing these forests. The master plan also decreed that women and the poor be included in the community forest user groups, and positioned forestry staff as advisers to these groups. With this, community forestry began; and would go on to become one of the most successful policies of the government of Nepal.

The Annapurna Conservation Area Project—ACAP—was conceived of in this context. According to an interview that Chandra gave to Hum Bahadur Gurung just a few months before his death, ACAP began with a paper co-authored by two American environmentalists, Michael Wright and Bruce Bunting, on the possibility of launching a model conservation project in the Annapurna area. The Nepali tourism entrepreneur Karna Shakya—credited with starting Kathmandu's tourist district, Thamel, by establishing the low-budget Kathmandu Guest House there—was at the time proposing that the Annapurna area be converted into a multiple-use recreational area. Tourism was already a major industry in the area. Environmentalists were worried that any expansion of the tourism industry would lead to the depletion of the Annapurna area. The trust was interested in finding a way to address both needs: the need for tourism (or for an increased income through tourism) and the need for nature conservation.

In 1985, Michael Wright and Bruce Bunting jointly presented a paper titled 'Annapurna National Park' at a seminar inaugurated by King Birendra, and presided over by Prince Gyanendra. 'At that time, once Prince Gyanendra thought the proposal was genuine, it was easy to work,' Chandra said in his interview to Hum Bahadur Gurung. Soon after the seminar, Hemanta Mishra—adept royal handler—organized a visit to the Annapurna area for King Birendra, at the end of which the king issued a royal directive to conserve the area. From this directive flowed the necessary finances: the World Wildlife Fund stepped in with $25,000 for a feasibility study.

Mingma Norbu Sherpa, Chandra and Broughton Coburn, an American consultant who had remained in Nepal following a stint in the Peace Corps, started the feasibility study in 1986. In the interview he gave, Chandra gleefully recalled being paid $700—enough to pay for meals at Nanglo, then the most popular restaurant in Kathmandu. 'There were no terms of reference,' he exclaimed in amazement. Within the team, Mingma was focused on conservation. Chandra's focus was on people's participation. Broughton Coburn's interest— according to Chandra—was on micro-hydropower as a means to the environmentally sustainable development of the Annapurna area.

They toured the area at the start of the study, beginning in the village of Lumle, and walking on to the villages of Ghandruk, Ghorepani, Tatopani, through lower Mustang District, and, over the Thorung Pass, to Manang District. By then the 'around Annapurna circuit' had become a heavily trekked route—second only to the Everest base camp trek, which saw some 40,000 trekkers a year. Yet the economic benefit to the area was negligible. And the environmental hazards were apparent.

Chandra, who had first visited Ghandruk in 1969, when he found it 'beautiful and well disciplined', was shocked to now find it squalid, with poor trails, and lodges so rudimentary as to discourage trekkers from staying overnight. There was no set rate for any of the services that the lodges provided. Bargain-hunting, low-budget trekkers would refuse to pay even a single rupee for accommodation; and desperate lodge owners would offer rooms for free if the trekkers would only eat there. On an earlier visit to Ghorepani, Chandra had seen a dense jungle in nearby Ulleri, so thick that people were afraid to walk through for fear of encountering bears. By now half the forests were gone.

Yet any talk of conservation immediately raised local anxiety. Nobody wanted their area to be declared a national park. 'By definition,' Chandra said in his interview, 'a national park means that you have to remove people, no one can live there.' Millions of people were living in the Annapurna area; they had millions of livestock. 'So what to do?'

The concept of a 'conservation area' came to clarity during the tour. A conservation area is synonymous with the more usual term 'protected area'. People would be allowed to continue living in it. There would be no armed protection for their forests. Instead, the people of the area would be enlisted to form community forest users groups, and trained—and entrusted—to manage their own forests. These groups (with the inelegant yet unavoidable acronym CFUG) would be allowed to set their own restrictions on the use of firewood, fodder and timber, and regulate hunting and poaching. Once they saw that conservation served their interests (by preserving resources for household consumption and by retaining the beauty of their area, which would in turn encourage tourism), they would become home-grown environmentalists. This, in brief, was the thinking behind ACAP.

Coming up with a brilliant scheme is one thing; implementing it brilliantly, quite another. Chandra, a local, put an inordinate amount of effort into the feasibility study, travelling more extensively than the other team members, and returning alone with the proposal to try to win local support for it. In an unusual move, he made the proposal for ACAP public. 'Very transparent...very open!' he exclaimed with typical enthusiasm in the interview he gave. This move helped to allay local fears that ACAP was a national park. It also helped sell the concept of ACAP to bureaucrats and government officials. In Kathmandu, the trust—ACAP's parent organization—also provided all the necessary backup. Hemanta Mishra saw to it that Prince Gyanendra approved the proposal. The World Wildlife Fund committed one million dollars for the following five years. The Annapurna Conservation Area Project was on.

ACAP launched in 1986 with a pilot project in Ghandruk, a picturesque Gurung village that fell on the 'around Annapurna circuit'. Mingma Norbu Sherpa, as ACAP's first director, decided not only to base the headquarters in Ghandruk, but to live there as well: an unusual decision in a country where a non-government organization's 'hakim sahib', or boss, usually works and lives in comfort, away from the project area.

Ghandruk was at the time a two-day walk from Pokhara, with an overnight stop at the village of Chandrakot. (It is now a few hours' walk from the Pokhara-Baglung highway, on which Chandrakot is but a fleeting bus stop.) The village had no electricity, no telephones, no large, modern buildings—just a huddle of traditional Gurung houses perched along a ridge overlooking Mt Machhapuchare.

Hum Bahadur Gurung, hired as a project assistant, accompanied Mingma to Ghandruk at the outset. 'We were there on day one,' he said, talking to me on Skype from Australia, where he was pursuing a PhD. Originally from Siklis, Hum was a soaltee of Chandra. He had been working as a personal assistant to the minister of law and justice, Radheshyam Kamaro—to whom Chandra would later turn for advice on his divorce—when Chandra told him about a job opening at ACAP.

'We rented Gopal's uncle's house—the rent was three hundred rupees a month,' Hum told me, laughing at the memory. There were only four staff members at the start. 'We swept the floor, and had a signboard made.'

According to Ghana Shyam Gurung (Ghurmet), who worked at ACAP before joining WWF, this was the first of ACAP's three main phases, the 'establishment phase'. The second phase began after Mingma left for the University of Michigan as a Fulbright scholar, to create a plan for environmental education in Nepal. Chandra was then appointed the director of ACAP.

Though Chandra had stumbled into conservation—and was an accidental environmentalist—he put all his heart into the work. 'I am not intelligent,' he told an American consultant, Maureen DeCoursey, during this time. 'But I work very hard.'

The chance to do something for his people energized Chandra; he was, after all, 'Kanchha Mukhiya' from Siklis. This was his chance to do something for his people. Equally, his being a local energized the people of Ghandruk. 'Dr Sah'b's being from that area helped ACAP to take off,' Ghana said, reminiscing about ACAP. With boyish enthusiasm, Chandra spread his can-do, bhaihaalchha, spirit throughout Ghandruk. Most of ACAP's work—the work that earned it worldwide acclaim—took place under Chandra's leadership. It was a period of hard work, innovation and plentiful funding. 'This,' said Ghana, 'was ACAP at its height.'

The work began small, though, with almost no mention of conservation. 'We did not talk about nurseries, we did not talk about plantations or community forestry,' Chandra said in his interview with Hum. Instead, he focused on small-scale development projects, which went by the rubric of 'community development'. None of the government-built drinking-water taps in Ghandruk were working at the time; the contractors had siphoned off the budgets, and the taps had all broken down soon after their construction. The first thing ACAP did was to build a good, reliable drinking-water tap in the village.

'It's still working, it's still working perfectly,' Hum told me over Skype. 'And it cost us only forty thousand rupees. The rest of the cost was raised from the village.'

Chandra had made 'people's participation' the organization's rallying cry, and it worked. Instead of telling the people of the area what to do, he wanted ACAP staff to solicit their opinions, and—unless their ideas clashed with broad conservation goals—to allow them to set the agenda for ACAP's work. But the people of the area also had to contribute—in cash or kind, or by donating their labour for free—towards each project, as a sign of their commitment. For example, if they wanted a village trail repaired, they had to raise a contribution (in cash or in labour) from each household. Only then would ACAP assist—with matching funds, or with engineering know-how. If people wanted the village school improved or expanded, they had to raise part of the expenses; then ACAP would make a matching donation. The thinking behind 'people's participation' was that people would have a sense of ownership if they contributed to development schemes; they would take care of them afterwards. This became a formula in later years: if people were willing to pitch in, ACAP would approve the project. At the start, though, especially for Chandra, this was a very personal mission. He wanted to invoke pride in his people: the pride he felt about his identity as a Gurung. He wanted them to do things for themselves instead of always looking to the government. Well before the janajati rights movement took hold, well before 'decentralization' and 'federalization' became popularized as slogans, Chandra set about effecting local autonomy through ACAP. He wanted to challenge his people to take charge of their area.

Chandra's mode of operation, from the start, was person-to-person contact. For ACAP staff, this meant an inordinate amount of what, in the world of non-government organizations, is summarily called 'mobilizing'. 'We met all the old folks of the village, we went to every house, we went door to door, we spent all our time talking,' Hum recalled to me over Skype. Laughing, he said that Chandra spent three years doing just that. Chandra's being a 'big person'—a PhD—gave him immense local credibility. And being the 'Kanchha Mukhiya' of Siklis gave him access to all the most influential village leaders. Yet the social dynamics of each village varied; he had to negotiate each one delicately. Ghandruk, at that time, had three leaders, three centres of power: the elected local official, Dilman Gurung; another village elder, Tek Bahadur Gurung; and the village mukhiya, Min Bahadur Gurung. 'Although Dilman was the official leader,' Chandra said in his interview to Hum, 'the major decision-maker was Min Bahadur. So we had to identify him, and talk to him, get his blessings.'

In Hum's words, this was extremely important: 'This was how we earned social capital.'

They later spent this capital promoting conservation. When the staff actually began conservation work, they did so carefully, allowing the community forest users groups—which in ACAP were more informally called 'conservation committees'—to make all the decisions about their forests, right or wrong. The committees then learned from their successes and failures. In the interview, Chandra noted: 'The committees developed their own rules and regulations, and if you read their minutes, they have made some very interesting decisions.' He took an example of an early rule passed by Ghandruk's conservation committee: everyone in the village was allowed to cut up to five trees a year to meet their timber, firewood and fodder needs. But, even while observing this quota, some people began to cut mature trees, while others would cut young, immature trees. The latter hampered the regeneration of the forests. 'They soon realized that the forests would be cleared due to their decision,' Chandra said. The committee amended the rule, banning the cutting of immature trees. In this way, the local people learned how to pass environment-friendly regulations.

The strategy succeeded, the work proved popular, and soon the organization was expanding, opening new offices in the villages of Lwang, Bhujung, Siklis...

THE BEST THING IN MY LIFE

It was around then, in 1990, that I met Chandra. Aged twenty-one, I had returned to Nepal from the United States, armed with a bachelor of fine arts in photography, for what I thought would be a few months before returning to the United States for graduate school. I was casting about for work in the interim. I went to meet Hemanta Mishra, a family acquaintance, to see if the King Mahendra Trust for Nature Conservation had any use for someone like me. It did not; but he passed on my résumé to Chandra, who hired me on a short assignment to set up a display on ACAP's work in its headquarters in Ghandruk.

I did not realize, till later, that the trust had just passed through a jittery time. In 1990, the People's Movement had ended the Panchayat regime, and restored democracy to the country. The standing of the monarchy was at an all-time low; and the standing of all organizations affiliated with the royal family, including the trust, had suffered as a consequence. There had been some talk of stripping the trust of its quasi-government status. This did not happen, however, as the democratic parties, in particular the Nepali Congress Party and the Communist Party of Nepal (Unified Marxist Leninist), proved more accommodating to the royal family than expected. The trust remained as it had been, with King Birendra its patron, and Prince Gyanendra its chairman.

Having overcome these jitters, ACAP was, at the time, about to have King Birendra inaugurate its headquarters in Ghandruk. My small assignment was timed for this. The office in Ghandruk had a display room that I was to design. It was not much of a job; but I was glad for it, and for the chance to get out of Kathmandu, into the countryside.

Chandra cut an immensely charismatic figure in Ghandruk: simultaneously a local leader and a worldly PhD, a villager and an internationalist, a son of the soil and an iconoclast, a leader, a thinker, a hippie, an activist. He was also extremely good-looking. He exuded physical confidence and had a winning, confiding manner. It was in Chandra's nature to constantly woo support—not by exhorting people to join his cause, but by working hard, and playing hard, and offering them a chance to join in. In between, he discussed bracing issues, asked questions, gossiped, shared colourful anecdotes and bawdy tales. He could make Ghandruk feel like the centre of the universe.

The consultant Maureen DeCoursey, who worked with him around this time, called Chandra a 'thunderbolt of a man'. Describing their work together, she emailed me from the United States: 'The many long walks through the hills (more than a few people thought he was my porter!), the marathon visits with the local folks, the late night debates over warm "teen pani raksi" (the best Gurung hooch you could get), and later, the articles we co-authored and the projects we dreamed up and implemented—these were the things that created a bond between us that made us like family.'

Chandra imparted that feeling to everyone: he even made me, working on the most minor of tasks, feel that ACAP—

and more than ACAP, the Annapurna area, the wildlife of Nepal, why, the earth itself—needed me. I had been starved for charismatic people in Kathmandu. And I had not, till Chandra, met a compatriot who was so global and simultaneously so—local. So very—Nepali. I, deracinated, had rejected everything about my background in order to become modern. He made me wonder if I need not have. He invoked an impossible nostalgia in me. He made me want to be more—Nepali. Or he brought to life the complex dynamics of the village, and made it legible to alienated urbanites like me.

I immediately developed a crush on him: I wanted to be like him. It was because of Chandra that I decided to live in Nepal. By the end of my brief stay in Ghandruk, he had got me talking to local women about women's development, he had tempted me (a teetotaller then) into drinking hot-lemon-and-rum (an ACAP staple), and he had got me uninhibited enough to sing and dance to folk songs whose words I did not know. Before I left, he asked me to join ACAP full-time to work in women's development. I had never, in my life, wanted to do such a thing. But so utterly convincing was Chandra that I found myself giving it serious consideration.

Yet I only joined ACAP two years later, when northern Mustang District came under its jurisdiction. Over dinner with a mutual friend in Kathmandu, Chandra had mentioned that he was having trouble finding anyone to work—and live—in the 'walled city' of Lo Monthang, near the Tibet border, a four days' walk from the nearest airport in Jomsom. Two candidates he had interviewed had refused the job. By then I had quit photography for writing, and had just published a travelogue to Lo Monthang. I could not resist; I asked Chandra to hire me. And Nepal was—it still is—like that: yet in-the-making, a bit unformed, its not-quite-set institutions allowed the confused (like myself at that age) to skip fields, to discover new interests, to dabble. In 1992, I set off to open ACAP's office in Lo Monthang, overseeing a staff of four. By the time I left in 1994, we had twenty-two staff working on projects in most of northern Mustang's twenty-six villages: establishing tree plantations and nurseries, building and repairing bridges and trails and river embankments, improving schools, supporting mothers' groups, running health camps, coordinating the restoration of monasteries. The experience stamped me, forever, in Chandra's mould.

Sink or swim: that was my experience, and the experience of most of ACAP's staff, who were, as Ghana Shyam Gurung (Ghurmet) put it, smiling wistfully, 'All energy, no experience.' After they were hired, the staff would, if lucky—which I was not—serve a brief apprenticeship in Ghandruk. Then they were left on their own to fulfil their contracts, the 'terms of reference' for which were, more often than not, vague. (For the concept of a conservation area was still evolving, and ACAP's mandate was not quite clear.) Any sound idea would win Chandra's immediate approval. Funds were never a problem. This gave the staff—ambitious twenty- and thirty-somethings—astounding power in the areas where they worked.

'You had full responsibility,' was how my former colleague Dibya Gurung put it. She said, 'You could do whatever you wanted—the strategy, the programme, was all up to you.'

Hired to head the women's development programme, Dibya spent a month in Ghandruk, learning, among other things, that singing and dancing—taking part in local festivities— were an essential part of her job. Her predecessor, Samita Bhattarai, had already initiated some programmes in women's development. One such programme was to set up mothers' groups—one of Chandra's favourite programmes at ACAP. There were mothers' groups in Ghandruk, but Dibya recalled that they were split into factions. When, overcoming their differences, they began to raise money to make foot trails, each group's success spurred the others. 'It was like there was a wave of work,' Dibya recalled. The pride that people felt about their accomplishments was infectious. 'The mothers' groups didn't just make trails—they planted trees, they made toilets, they cleaned up the villages. Even in Dalit villages, the mothers wanted to prove themselves, and they did.'

Dibya was then sent off to the office in Lwang, with little instruction about how to proceed. No one was at the office in Lwang. Plans were under way to build a micro-hydropower plant, and Siddhartha Bajra Bajracharya, who headed the office, was out on this work. When he came back, Dibya took a round of the villages with him, but continued to flounder. 'It was difficult to know what we were supposed to do,' she said. 'And there was resistance to women officers among the male staff. There was no gender sensitivity training, they didn't want to see us as equals.'

Wider resistance to the women's development programme came from among the local men. 'The mothers' groups went vertically, women hadn't been mainstreamed,' Dibya told me, using the jargon of the development world. This meant that women were segregated from 'men's work'—there were only two women in each conservation committee—and men were segregated from the mothers' groups. 'But gender means everyone, not just women.' Dibya and Jagan Subba Gurung, a young woman from Ghandruk who had been hired to work on women's development, decided to involve the local men in the mothers' groups.

She had thought Chandra would be pleased with her progress, but when he came to the office in Lwang a month later, the first thing he did was berate her. 'It was a Saturday, a day off,' Dibya recalled. 'I hadn't done up my hair, and I was wearing tights. Not just tights: extremely colourful tights, you know. When he saw me he exploded: "Put your hair up! Put on something else! How will the local women ever respect you if you look like this?"'

As 'Kanchha Mukhiya', Chandra was fierce in enforcing local respectability. And there was a side of him the staff dreaded: the micromanager. Determined to do everything properly, he could not tolerate even the slightest hint of sloppiness from the staff. His nephew Krishnaman Gurung told me that Chandra was finicky about his own appearance as well: 'It was hard to find clothes in his size, because he was so tall. And he wore only the best.' When his staff displeased him, he did not hesitate to let his ire show.

'He would scold us as though we were children,' said Siddhartha Bajra Bajracharya, recalling exactly this trait of his. Chandra mentored the staff on the smallest matters, from how to walk to how to conduct home visits. 'He even worried about what we wore.' Siddhartha echoed some of Chandra's words to him: 'Why haven't you combed your hair? Don't you have proper shoes? You're dressed like a porter! Don't you have better clothes to wear?'

As for work, Chandra let the staff set their own agendas. He devolved responsibility completely. 'He trusted the staff a hundred per cent,' said Tara Gurung, who had been ACAP's agro-forestry specialist. 'He trusted everyone.'

Siddhartha agreed. He told me that before he headed the Lwang office, he had conducted mobile lodge-management training sessions all over the Annapurna area, including at the base of the Thorung-la pass, in Manang District. 'We trained every single hotel in Manang,' he said. 'This was in the monsoon. There were landslides everywhere. There were no flights. We spent a week in each village, teaching the hotels how to standardize their menus, how to cook.' The International Labour Organization had funded that work. The Lwang office, he said, focused on agro-forestry with funding from the Netherlands Development Organisation. 'They told us it was one of their most successful projects.'

'Dr Sah'b gave us a free hand,' Shailendra Thakali told me. Shailendra had worked on conservation education before going on to head the Ghandruk office. Chandra, he said, did not just train him professionally: he had also taught him life lessons. He was not a boss, but a mentor. In an obituary that Shailendra wrote, he mentioned that Mingma Norbu Sherpa and Chandra had shaped him all his life.

Mingma and Chandra's most enduring legacy was, in fact, to mentor a generation of environmentalists, a generation that with their passing went on to head the country's top conservation organizations. Mingma was particularly keen on conservation education. The work he did at the trust focused squarely on this. With Hemanta Mishra's support, he devised a programme to offer scholarships for study abroad in parks and recreation and wildlife management. This, while ACAP was in the planning phase. These scholarships filled an important gap; while forestry was by then an established field of study in Nepal, conservation still was not. There just were not enough environmentalists in Nepal to fill the jobs that an organization such as ACAP was going to create.

Most of the candidates that the trust gave scholarships to came—like Mingma and Chandra—from rural areas. Shailendra Thakali, born in the town of Jomsom, in Mustang District, won a scholarship to study at the Lincoln University, New Zealand. Lal Prasad Gurung had been working as a research assistant at the Lumle Agricultural Centre when Chandra, Mingma and Broughton Coburn came by on ACAP's feasibility study. He learned about the same scholarship from them, and, upon applying, won it. Nima Sherpa, originally from the eastern hills, also won a scholarship. Ghana Shyam Gurung (Ghurmet), originally from the village of Dhee in northern Mustang, was only the second person from his district to pass high school in the first division. He learned about the scholarship from a chance meeting with Mingma, and also won it upon applying.

As with the recipients of these scholarships, the staff that Mingma and Chandra hired at ACAP tended to be from ethnic/indigenous groups originally from outside Kathmandu; most were native to the Annapurna area. Their surnames alone revealed so: Dibya Gurung, Hum Bahadur Gurung, Tara Gurung, Devi Gurung, Tshering Lama, Ang Phuri

Sherpa, Gehendra Gurung...This hiring policy proved immensely popular locally; the local people felt completely at ease with the ACAP staff. But from early on, this became a bone of contention at the trust, a Kathmandu institution through and through. For even after democracy in 1990, the trust remained staunchly part of the Kathmandu establishment, manned overwhelmingly by bureaucrats of the Bahun and Chettri castes, and by Newars from the Kathmandu valley. Janajatis from outside Kathmandu were rank outsiders there.

Murmuring snidely about communalism, the trust's staff dubbed ACAP 'AGAP', the 'Annapurna Gurung Advancement Project'. Chandra made light of the charge. The entire point of ACAP, he argued, was to develop local capacity in conservation; how could one do so with staff from Kathmandu? He always gave preference to locals, and hired outsiders only as a last resort.

Siddhartha Bajra Bajracharya, born and bred in Kathmandu, applied for a job at ACAP while doing his postgraduate studies in zoology and ecology at the University of Edinburgh. Chandra refused to even interview him at first. 'He didn't believe that a Kathmandu Newar could work in an area like that,' Siddhartha recalled. 'He kept saying, "Annapurna is a difficult area. You have to be able to cross the Thorung-la pass. Can you do that?"' Fortunately, Hemanta Mishra proved more approachable. But even after Siddhartha was hired at ACAP, Chandra kept dismissing him: 'He would say, "Why are you here, go back to Kathmandu."' Terrified at first, he nevertheless stuck with the job; and withstanding the many upheavals that later shook ACAP and the trust, he rose through the ranks to head the trust. (By which time the King

Mahendra Trust for Nature Conservation had been renamed the National Trust for Nature Conservation, and all affiliation with the royal family had ended.)

Anil Manandhar—the WWF Country Representative after Chandra's passing—was also originally from Kathmandu. Like Siddhartha, he was hired at ACAP after completing his education, in both forestry and engineering, in Bulgaria. Perhaps because he was more implacable by temperament, he was less shaken by Chandra. But Kathmandu natives like him—and me—were in the minority at ACAP, which even we felt was rightful, just.

Eventually, ACAP had close to 200 staff, of whom almost 80 per cent were local—either from the Annapurna area, or from Pokhara and the vicinity. Spread all over the conservation area—summarily called the 'field'—they sometimes worked in their own offices, and at other times offered their expertise to the other offices.

The work could often be pell-mell. Chandra's ethic included non-stop work: to the alarm of the staff, he was often at the office at six in the morning, sipping tea. 'There were no office hours,' Tara Gurung recalled; for in a village, people made little distinction between personal and professional life. (Which made Saturdays and short holidays a dead loss for the staff.) Also, Chandra—separated from his wife and children—had no family life to speak of, not, at least, in the field. His family life, such as it was, was neatly tucked away in Kathmandu: only very few of the ACAP staff knew that he was married, and separated, with two children, no three, and a girlfriend in Japan, or maybe a wife, and not in Japan but in Nairobi, or maybe Jordan. Or maybe he had four children. This was one of Chandra's main paradoxes: though he was an utter extrovert, admired for his openness and candour, his work and family lives remained wholly segregated. In the field, he confided in no one about his family life. His work was his life. Holidays, or time off, were of no importance to him. He expected all his staff to be the same, and this often led to exhaustion. 'No one lasted long,' Dibya Gurung recalled. 'Everyone would eventually burn out.'

Running an organization was not, in fact, Chandra's forte. 'He was a visionary,' was how Dibya put it to me. 'He was definitely a leader, but he wasn't a manager.' In villages, work decisions were contingent on many variables—on the cooperation of the local people, on funding, on the availability of experts and even on the season. Everything could feel a bit ad hoc and unplanned. While this made what was called the 'programme side' of ACAP sensitive and responsive and extremely productive, it left the 'administration side'—the paperwork, the reporting, the documentation—perpetually scrambling to keep up.

Chandra paid hardly any mind to the administration side. But in the programme side, he had strict, if unwritten, rules that the staff had to follow. They were always to defer to the local people, to call them by terms of respect, like 'Aama' and 'Ba'—mother and father—and to fit into the cultural norms of the village. For female staff, this meant wearing local clothes. (The male staff, of course, just wore pants.) Before launching any scheme, the staff had to initiate village-wide dialogue. They had to woo the village leaders in particular—doing what one colleague laughingly recalled as 'performing prayers before all those old men'. At the same time, the staff had to watch out for the interests of those who wielded little power in the village: women, minorities, the Dalit castes, the poor. Once the village had decided on a scheme, the staff had to set up a committee to oversee the work and the local contribution towards it. Implementing the scheme was just half the job. The other half was reporting on it—in quarterly and annual reports, at annual meetings, and before donors who dropped by, which they often did, fitting in a trek along the way.

All the ACAP staff were constantly on the move, walking from village to village, or going to Pokhara, where the organization had opened an office to do work that could not be done out of Ghandruk—centralized purchasing, centralized auditing. All field offices had radio links, and the staff communicated daily with each other, and with staff at the trust, in Kathmandu. There was a constant exchange of experiences and ideas. Staff meetings—held annually in the head office in Ghandruk village—were full of excitement, edginess, revelry.

'It was like a family,' Dibya recalled. If so, it was a family with the usual share of rivalries: everyone was young, and ambitious, and keen to make this experience—in an organization that was growing in stature around the world—count. Jealousies flared up; personalities clashed, and working styles differed; the promotion of one set off the ambitions of all the others. The male staff felt that Chandra favoured the women, and the women felt that the men were hostile to them. (The men did, indeed, deride the women's development programme—WD—as the 'wakka-dikka' programme, or the 'sick and tired' programme.)

Still, the staff worked, and worked, and worked, setting up mothers' groups, improving schools, making micro-hydro projects to light up the villages, upgrading government health care facilities, promoting eco-trekking, building foot bridges, introducing conservation-friendly farming practices, encouraging vegetable farming to aid nutrition, establishing lodge-management committees to set standard prices for standard services to make trekking more financially beneficial...Chandra's can-do spirit touched all the ACAP staff. How many local people did the staff win over, how many village meetings did they hold, how many donors did they take to mothers' group meetings, to schools, to the jungles, to micro-hydropower plants? Every project ACAP launched proved a success.

ACAP was the envy of other NGOs—many of which paid their staff far more, but did not elicit such dedication. It was Chandra who inspired all this. 'What we did, we felt we had to do it for him,' Dibya said to me, expressing a sentiment that I had also shared. In Kathmandu, the trust was able to get the government to authorize ACAP to collect 'entry fees' from trekkers to fund its work. This was unlike any non-government organization in Nepal. 'It was like a super-ministry,' commented Ghana Shyam Gurung (Ghurmet). 'It did everything except build large dams and dig for oil. There's nothing ACAP didn't do.'

Said Dibya wistfully, 'It was the best thing in my life.'

Yes, but what did it do for the local ecology? In my own office, in northern Mustang, ACAP did relatively little in terms of nature conservation. When opening the area for tourism in 1992, the government had banned trekking groups from using local natural resources; so we did not have to worry about the environmental impact of tourism. There were no forests in that arid steppe; hence we could set up no conservation committees. The surrounding scrublands and pasturelands were quite eroded, but regenerating them was a difficult, and expensive, proposition. A USAID project had tried to do just this in southern Mustang in the 1970s, and failed, to much local notoriety. We did not want to repeat the experiment. We did help to establish depots for subsidized kerosene, to encourage the local people to stop cutting shrubs to use as kindling in the local goat-pellet-fuelled stoves. And we helped to subsidize the cost of solar panels, though this provided energy enough only for lighting, and not for cooking. We helped to establish nurseries in almost every village, but the species that proved the most feasible met only timber needs. Later, the American Himalayan Foundation stepped in with funds for a micro-hydro plant in Lo Monthang, but again, this only lit up the village; it did not meet cooking needs. There was, in truth, little we could do in northern Mustang. We did it. Then we turned to culture conservation; and indeed, enabling the restoration of two fifteenth-century monasteries in Lo Monthang by the American Himalayan Foundation became one of ACAP's major achievements in the area.

From talking to former ACAP colleagues I discovered that this was, fortunately, not a typical experience. In the rest of the Annapurna area, ACAP's focus was solidly on nature conservation. The Annapurna area is home to over 101 mammalian species, 472 species of bird, twenty-one species of amphibian and thirty-two species of reptile. A study conducted in 2004 found a significantly lower mean density of cut tree stumps inside the conservation area than immediately outside it, indicating lower timber, firewood and fodder use inside. While the density of tree cover was the same inside and outside the conservation area, they found a greater diversity of species inside: forty-three species, as compared to twenty-three outside. The study also found that the wildlife population of the area had increased following the establishment of ACAP. Additionally, the people of the area felt more able to protect the wildlife from external poachers and hunters. Launched as a model conservation project, ACAP had, thus, lived up to its vision. And yet barely a decade after its launch, it had already come undone.

IT WAS THE ASSOCIATION WITH THE ROYAL FAMILY

In Siklis, Chandra's stature had just risen and risen. 'He was very powerful,' recalled Ghana Shyam Gurung (Ghurmet), who headed ACAP's office in Siklis. 'The people of the village welcomed him like a hero when he visited.' Chandra had always brought ideas and energy to the village—and now, through ACAP, he also brought money. 'Kanchha Mukhiya' had done his people proud. 'If people wanted anything, they'd go directly to him,' Ghana said. They also went straight to him with complaints. Laughing, Ghana said he found this level of accountability extremely bracing.

During Ghana's years in Siklis, ACAP's focus was on electrification. Micro-hydropower had been on the agenda since ACAP's inception. MIT-trained engineer Bikash Pandey, who then worked at a private company, DCS, in the town of Butwal, first met Chandra in 1986, when Chandra asked the company to conduct a feasibility survey in Siklis. This was when Chandra had yet to complete his PhD in Hawaii. 'He wasn't like a Nepali—at first I thought he was a gora-saheb,' Bikash told me. When he went to Siklis to conduct the survey, Chandra accompanied him. Bikash was impressed by how warmly people greeted them in the village. He was also struck by Chandra. 'You could see he really wanted to do something,' he said. Bikash found that it would be possible to build an environmentally safe and economically low-cost scheme with parts made in Nepal.

A few years later, when Chandra was heading ACAP in Ghandruk, he invited DCS to conduct a feasibility survey there, and, once again, in Siklis. Even before the surveys were completed, Chandra had secured funding for these plants. During their construction he again turned to Bikash for help. By this time Bikash had joined the Intermediate Technology Development Group—a non-government organization that followed E. F. Schumacher's philosophy of 'small is beautiful'. Chandra asked Bikash to serve as ACAP's 'energy adviser', overseeing the construction of these hydropower schemes, looking out for the welfare of the people.

'The pipes that DCS used for Ghandruk were made during the 1990 People's Movement,' Bikash told me. In the previous year, India had imposed an embargo on Nepal; the necessary materials had not all been available. 'The quality wasn't up to standard,' Bikash explained. In Ghandruk, during a trial run of the scheme, one of the pipes burst; Chandra and four other people were thrown several metres by the force of the explosion.

No one was hurt, but everyone was badly shaken. Chandra's reaction was quite unexpected. 'There was a belief in the village that if you suffer a fright, you lose your saato,' Bikash told me. Saato perhaps best translates as 'spirit'. After the explosion, Chandra was convinced that he had lost his saato. 'At first I thought he was just going along with what the villagers were saying,' Bikash said to me. 'But he was quite serious about it. He stopped smiling, he stopped laughing. He wasn't himself any more.'

Following local custom, Chandra wore unrefined threads to get his saato back, and sprinkled water on a chicken to see if his saato had returned. (If the chicken shrugged, this was a sign that the saato had returned.) The chicken did not shrug. Not until Chandra got to Pokhara, where his sister Humkali had a special ritual performed at her house, did he feel normal again. Humkali had told me about this when I had met her in Pokhara: 'I cradled his head in my arms, I said syau, syau, syau,' (a sound meant to call back the spirit). 'I said, my younger brother's saato has gone, we need to bring it back. I fetched a jhaankri'—a shaman.

The ritual apparently restored Chandra's saato. It had taken two weeks. 'I was really surprised,' Bikash recalled. 'You'd think he was modern, but then he had this—other side.'

Back at work, Chandra asked Bikash to negotiate some compensation on behalf of the people of Ghandruk. And he did. DCS eventually replaced all the pipes, and, to make amends for a six-month delay in the construction of the micro-hydro plant, provided a diesel generator to electrify Ghandruk provisionally.

'And the light was so weak you had to shine a flashlight on the bulb just to see it!' These are words I remember Chandra saying, amid uproarious laughter, over dinner in Ghandruk. (He was being facetious: the lights in Ghandruk were not, in fact, so weak.)

The Ghandruk micro-hydro plant was inaugurated in 1990, not by King Birendra or Prince Gyanendra (as they might have expected), but by Prime Minister Girija Prasad Koirala, in a clear embracing of democracy—something Chandra would pay for dearly in the coming years. The inauguration was conducted with much fanfare. 'They had four helicopters bringing everyone in,' remembered Bikash, who was there for the occasion. 'This fondness he had for helicopters...' He shook his head. 'He really liked to do things big.'

Ghana Shyam Gurung (Ghurmet) personally oversaw the electrification of Ghale Gaon, Tangting and Khilang villages. So many years later, he still spoke of this accomplishment with pride: 'Children got to study at night, at last. People became more productive. Income levels went up.' The use of forest resources decreased as ACAP introduced electric pots—bijuli dekchi—with which people could heat water. ACAP also helped to establish kerosene depots, making it possible for people to use kerosene instead of firewood for cooking, thereby protecting the forests. The village was earning money from the campsites along the route to Ghale Gaon. Before leaving, Ghana also helped to establish a forest nursery in Siklis.

When he did leave, he was sent off in grand style by the villagers. 'They put so many garlands on me, they came all the way down to my feet,' he said. They presented him with eighteen raadis—woollen rugs—as mementos of the village, and on the day he left, they gave him a grand send-off with music played by the local musicians. 'The villagers from Khilang, Tangting, Yangjakot—they all came to see me off,' he said to me, not without a touch of defiance.

This defiance, because ACAP had begun to encounter some opposition by then. Two offices, in particular, were being targeted: mine, in Lo Monthang, and Ghana's, in Siklis. An unnamed litigant had filed a complaint against my office, accusing us of having bought wood from an unauthorized contractor and promoting deforestation as part of a monastery renovation project. A case was also filed against Ghana's office in Siklis, alleging financial irregularities in the construction of the building that housed the micro-hydro plant. Both charges were eventually dropped—but not before causing years of heartache to the staff named in the suits, who became hostage to drawn-out legal proceedings.

'It was the association with the royal family,' Ghana reminisced, explaining the opposition as he had come to understand it with many years' hindsight. Democrats who opposed the royal family assumed the worst of the trust: unfairly, they saw its projects, like ACAP, as being little more than vehicles for Prince Gyanendra.

And there was also opposition to ACAP within the trust. ACAP was just one of the trust's projects, but so successful was it that it attracted all the attention—and funding. It overshadowed the remaining projects at the trust. Though Chandra eventually left Ghandruk to work as Hemanta Mishra's right-hand man at the trust, dividing his time between ACAP and the trust's other projects, he was always associated with AGAP—the 'Annapurna Gurung Advancement Project'. A janajati. He was an outsider.

He was also uncomfortable with the ways of the royal court. When Hemanta Mishra left the trust to join the World Bank in Washington, DC, Chandra replaced him provisionally as the head of the trust. Chandra was no royal handler. I remember clearly his amazement at the extent to which he was now expected to bow and scrape before Prince Gyanendra. 'They thought I'd come to his palace every morning, whether or not there was work, just to pay homage,' he once told a group of staff. At the time, anyone entering the prince's palace had to wear the national dress—which, for men, amounted to a labeda-sural, a jacket, and a woven Dhaka topi. Chandra kept a cleaned and pressed pair ready in his office; and he did go to Prince Gyanendra's palace, often at short notice, when there was work. But he did not participate in the feudal custom of chaakadi, where supplicants spent their mornings in their patron's court, praising him and pandering to his whims. Hemanta Mishra, Chandra discovered, had gone to meet Prince Gyanendra almost every day. Chandra did not want to do this. Nor did he feel welcome to do so. With the ACAP staff, he puzzled, 'Should I be going there every morning? What do you think? Should I go?'

He also shared other dilemmas with the staff. One such dilemma was a request from Prince Gyanendra to organize a hunting trip to northern Mustang. The request came in 1992, just as the area was being added to the conservation area. Chandra was told that Prince Gyanendra wanted to hunt for snow leopard. In a throwback to the days of the royal shikar, the trust was asked to organize the hunt.

In a quandary, Chandra convened a meeting of trust staff. At that time I had just signed on to work in northern Mustang. I sat in on the meeting. To the mind of even a neophyte like me, there was no question of supporting such a hunt. According to Rodney Jackson, who has studied this elegant, elusive big cat, there are only about 6,000 snow leopards left in the wild, in the alpine and sub-alpine regions of Central Asia, from Bhutan in the east to India and Nepal, Pakistan and Afghanistan, into China, Kazakhstan, Kyrgystan,

Tajikistan, Uzbekistan, Mongolia and Russia. Of these, 350 to 500 live in northern Nepal. Environmentalists see the snow leopard as a flagship species, an indicator of the health of the local ecology. Hunting them was unthinkable.

Yet—so unreformed was the royal palace—it was also unthinkable to refuse a request by Prince Gyanendra. In this case, Chandra was obliged to do so. I remember the morning he went to Prince Gyanendra's palace, decked in official gear, to dissuade him from the hunt. Chandra was nervous, joking: 'I hope they're not going to kill me, au!' When he returned to the office, he looked relieved. I asked him how it had gone. The prince, he told me, had just listened to him, and agreed to abide by his decision. 'I didn't know if I was going to come back alive,' he joked again. 'But he didn't say anything, he just listened.' He felt he had passed a crucial test.

He had not. Laxmibadan Maskey's *Tiger Warden* has chronicled the extreme servility that the royal family expected from those whom they felt they were patronizing. Right up to the abolition of monarchy in Nepal, the royal family expected conservationists to put aside all other work to cater to their whims.

This expectation extended to Laxmibadan Maskey's husband even when Tirtha Man Maskey reached the height of his career, as the director general of the Department of National Parks and Wildlife Conservation. In 2001, Gyanendra ascended from prince to king upon the massacre of his brother King Birendra and all other heirs. Four years later, he took over in an ill-advised attempt to revive an absolute monarchy. Shortly thereafter, he had Tirtha Man Maskey accompany him on an official visit to several African states. Laxmibadan Maskey writes that during this trip, among other duties, her late husband had to take the queens shopping. (For this, King Gyanendra tipped Tirtha Man Maskey a hundred dollars.) She writes that throughout his long association with the royal family, Tirtha Man Maskey had put up with private humiliations—like being offered ice cream that King Gyanendra had eaten, something most Hindus would consider extremely offensive. For his association with the royal family, he was tarred as a royalist: a legal case was filed against him in the Commission for the Investigation of the Abuse of Authority. (By then, the same had happened to Chandra.) Yet, for all the loyalty Tirtha Man Maskey had shown the royal family, little loyalty was returned. Of her husband's death, Laxmibadan Maskey writes: 'The king didn't send a single condolence. While he was alive, he took his work, after he died, they forgot him.'

This was the kind of 'service' that Gyanendra—then just a prince—had expected of Chandra as the head of the trust. But Chandra—the son of a mukhiya—was too proud to scrape and grovel. Also, the times were changing; Nepal had, after all, a democratic polity in which the political parties, rather than the royal family, held power. For the sake of the trust's survival, it was important to forge links with democratic leaders. It was untenable to remain a servant of the royal court.

As Ghana saw it, Prince Gyanendra began to see Chandra as uppity, ungrateful, after Chandra invited Prime Minister Girija Prasad Koirala, instead of the prince, to inaugurate a new micro-hydro plant in the village of Birethanti. 'Gyanendra loved to inaugurate things,' Ghana reminisced. 'He just couldn't understand why the prime minister was invited.' To add insult to injury, in 1994, *Asiaweek* ran a profile on Chandra, valourizing him as the son of a village chief who was serving his people well. Charismatic Chandra was overshadowing the prince. Over his years at the trust, Chandra had won not just Nepali government awards—the Prabal Gorkha Dakshin Bahu, the Mahendra Bidya Bhusan, the Birendra Aishwarya Sewa Padak—but also, along with Gyanendra, an Order of the Golden Ark from the Netherlands. Perhaps Gyanendra felt he was being sidelined. 'He always wanted to be in the limelight,' said Ghana.

How Chandra left the trust—or how he was made to leave—exposed the cross-purposes at which Nepali environmentalists ultimately were in seeking royal patronage. To lay the grounds for Chandra's dismissal, Prince Gyanendra's loyalists in the trust began to leak ACAP documents to the media, spreading word of the lawsuits against the offices in Siklis and Lo Monthang. This fuelled public speculation about corruption at ACAP. Its spotless image was being sullied. But worse than that was the knowledge, among the ACAP staff, that their own colleagues in the trust were out to destroy the organization. The ACAP staff felt besieged. For though they knew that there had been no corruption in the organization, they knew, too, that the administration side—the paperwork—was weak. Such paperwork was crucial in legal defence. I asked Hari Gopal Shrestha, who looked after the trust's accounts during Chandra's time, about the way the cases were dismissed. 'There was no financial mishandling. It was all political. It was all envy,' he said, adding, 'but because the focus was all in the field, there were weaknesses in the paperwork. The focus was on making the project a success. And there was a lot of work, good work, which brought real returns to the people. But...in government organizations, there's more attention to paperwork.'

The atmosphere within the trust grew poisoned as Chandra's term as its provisional head neared its end, in 1995. The question of who would next head the trust was an ever-present topic of gossip. To the ACAP staff, it seemed obvious that Chandra's term should be renewed: his work in ACAP had brought the trust unprecedented prestige, after all. But the trust staff preferred a Kathmandu insider, a royalist. Other environmentalists' names were also cropping up: Mingma Norbu Sherpa, who was then with WWF US, was one much-cited name. Tirtha Man Maskey was another. There was also speculation that Hemanta Mishra might return from the United States to resume his old position. The appointment was Prince Gyanendra's alone to make.

Chandra did not know, till the very end, what his fate was to be. In public he kept a bright facade, but with confidants he shared his growing anxiety. He kept trying to read Prince Gyanendra, to no avail: in their dealings the prince was all mask and no depth. Then, one day, the prince summoned Chandra to the eastern district of Jhapa, where he was on a visit. He told him that the job was his. 'It's yours, put in your application,' was what Chandra told his friends Prince Gyanendra told him in Jhapa. Chandra promptly did so, feeling assured at last. 'The palace told him—it's confirmed,' Hum Bahadur Gurung told me over Skype from Australia. 'We even went to see a cinema to celebrate,' he said.

But just a few days before the appointment was formalized, Prince Gyanendra summoned Chandra to his palace in Kathmandu, to tell him that he had given the job to someone else, after all. 'It's someone high-level, someone who's above it all,' is what Chandra reported Prince Gyanendra as having said: 'Don't worry, it's someone you'll have no problems with.' The prince did not say whom he had chosen.

Though disappointed, Chandra assumed that the prince had opted for a senior environmentalist. On the day of the appointment, however, Jaya Pratap Rana was named the trust's new head. A bureaucrat with no background in conservation, Jaya Pratap Rana was a royal relative: a palace insider, someone whose loyalty the prince clearly felt he could rely on. The Kathmandu establishment had reasserted its hold over the trust.

'You can't blame anyone but Gyanendra for what happened,' Ghana Shyam Gurung (Ghurmet) said to me, about Chandra's departure from the trust, and ACAP's, and the trust's, demise. 'Look at all the other trusts the royal family headed,' he said, naming the lacklustre Lumbini Development Trust and the ever-controversial Pashupati Development Trust. 'Where are they now?' he said hotly. If the King Mahendra Trust for Nature Conservation had alone shone under royal patronage, it was because of all the hard work Chandra had put into it after 1990. 'He maintained the trust's standard, its integrity,' Ghana said. 'But Gyanendra put his head on the chopping block.'

'You would never get a job like that if you lacked the culture of the palace,' commented soaltee Professor Jagman Gurung.

'It was like a takeover by the palace's Chettris and Bahuns and Newars,' was Bikash Pandey's explanation. 'At the trust, it was always them against the two janajatis,' he said, meaning Mingma Norbu Sherpa and Chandra.

With Jaya Pratap Rana's appointment, Chandra was demoted. There was nothing for it but to resign. He soon did.

THE BEWILDERMENT YEARS

Chandra's resignation from the trust was followed by that of many others at ACAP, for it was clear that the organization's best days were over. Ghana considered that this was when ACAP entered its third phase. The work continued, of course, but by rote, without inspiration. 'The work became like a ritual—or like an old machine, without lubricants,' he said. The trust began to exert more control on ACAP: it put a ceiling on its budget and diverted funds to other projects. ACAP's headquarters was moved out of Ghandruk village, to Pokhara. Its core concept—people's participation—became formulaic. 'There was no updating, there was no renewal,' said Ghana. Most disastrously, the trust stopped hiring local people. The new staff, from Kathmandu, had little feeling for the area, 'Then,' he continued, 'with the Maoists, things got out of hand. If we had been there, we might have saved the Ghandruk office. But—' He said, 'The connection to the people was lost.'

For his part, Chandra was stunned by the way Prince Gyanendra had manoeuvred him out of the trust. By that time I had left northern Mustang and returned to Kathmandu, to start a writing life. Whenever we met, Chandra would speculate endlessly about what had happened, why the prince had first said the job was his and then changed his mind, and whether the prince had intended to humiliate him. 'Could he be that petty?' he would speculate. And speculation it had to be, for Prince Gyanendra had never bothered to offer an explanation. 'Why did he tell me I had the job when I didn't have it?' Chandra would ask. 'Did he just say that, knowing I wouldn't get it? Or did he change his mind? Why didn't he tell me who it would be?' To family members he expressed his bitterest feelings: 'They tossed me out the way you'd toss a fly out of milk.'

He looked for another job, but Kathmandu was so small; not many non-government organizations had room for someone of his stature. For a year and a half he worked for a United Nations project on 'quality tourism'. The project was a success but his heart was not in it. For a while he went to Jordan to live with Tokiko Sato—but he could not abide by the thought of living abroad. Ghana told me, 'He wanted to come back. He just never wanted to do anything other than to work in Nepal.' Chandra still directed funds to the Annapurna area when he could. In 1996, while Bikash Pandey was pursuing studies at Berkeley, Chandra phoned him with news that he had found money from Japan, from the Tokoshima-Nepal Friendship Association, for a micro-hydropower plant in the village of Bhujung, in the Annapurna area.

By this time Chandra was married to Tokiko. Through his years at ACAP and the trust, he had visited her and their son Yoichi on every long holiday, in Nairobi and in Jordan, wherever Tokiko was working. When in Nepal, Chandra lived alone in a rented apartment in Mingma Norbu Sherpa's home. It was a cheery apartment, spacious and tasteful, but—such homebodies are Nepalis—Chandra's being a 'renter' only seemed to draw attention to the fact that he had no house of his own. This was extremely unusual for a man of his accomplishment. But Chandra had given up any claims on the house that his first wife, Sumitra, had built after their marriage. And his salary at the trust had been modest. Much of it had gone towards the education of his children Amanda and Adhish in the best private schools in Kathmandu. This, according to a childcare settlement between him and Sumitra. Chandra's main experience of fatherhood had been that of a provider. Though he often had Amanda and Adhish over to his apartment, he was so busy with work that he did not spend much time with them. Emotionally, though, he was devoted to them. He doted on his daughter Amanda, and while as a child Adhish had had some trouble relating to his father—he used to call Chandra 'Amanda's father'—they later developed a close bond. But for their mother Chandra had absolutely no affection. 'There was no confusion in his mind about whom he loved,' Bikash Pandey told me; and indeed, everyone I spoke to about his relationship with Tokiko said that it was deep and committed, and a source of great comfort to him. Yet Chandra's life with Tokiko took place almost entirely outside Nepal. Tokiko did come to visit a few times, staying

at Chandra's apartment and meeting his sister Humkali and ageing parents, Ratansingh and Krishnakumari. Chandra and she eventually had a second son, Eiki, whom many people I talked to called a 'duplicate' of his father, a 'photocopy'. Despite all this, Tokiko did not want to live in Nepal.

One obstruction was that Chandra was never able to obtain a divorce from Sumitra. By Nepali law there was little a man could do to initiate divorce from a wife with whom he had had children. This anachronistic Hindu law—passed to protect women from abandonment by their husbands—had been the bane of many an unhappily married man, who was left either to spend all his life in a loveless marriage or to marry a second wife illegally: commit bigamy.

This was what Chandra did. He did try not to; he tried, repeatedly, to obtain a divorce from Sumitra. But she repeatedly refused. 'For two or three years, he was always going to the courts,' Hum Bahadur Gurung said, recalling that period in Chandra's life. 'The rule, as it turned out, was that if the woman wants a divorce, it will happen. And by Newari custom, it's a difficult thing, to be a divorced woman.'

That was his explanation for why Sumitra had refused. Talking to me about it, Sumitra said, candidly enough, 'What would I get out of it?' She explained, 'The custody of the children would have gone to the father.' This was true. By another anachronistic Hindu law, fathers automatically won custody of children over the age of five. Sumitra said, 'I figured that if the children wanted, they could always go and visit him. Now that they're both grown, it's different,' she added. 'I could have granted him a divorce later on. But at that time they were too young.'

Was it true that Chandra had tried again and again, I asked.

'First he came with a paper, trying to establish a three-year separation,' she said. The document had been drafted on the advice of the former minister of law and justice, Radheshyam Kamaro. 'But I didn't want to sign it.' Her own focus was on preventing Chandra from marrying Tokiko Sato. She knew he could not do so without a divorce. 'And there's a law against bigamy,' Sumitra told me. A wife could annul her husband's second marriage if she reported it within thirty days of its taking place. She said, 'I was waiting for Tokiko to come to Nepal, so that I could report their marriage.'

But—foiling her—Chandra and Tokiko got married abroad. Sumitra discovered this only after the event. 'When he returned, I went to his office to drop off Amanda and Adhish, and he said, "Look, we got married, there's nothing you can do about it now."' He must have falsified documents from the village development committee—the local government body—to claim that he was unmarried, she said to me.

Chandra then proceeded to file for divorce through the village development committee. 'That paper never reached me,' Sumitra said. 'After that, he filed through the Kathmandu Municipality. We both had to appear in court.' She contested his claim that they were separated. In any case the law favoured her. Chandra's petition for divorce was denied.

Many people I spoke to lamented Sumitra's adamancy on this matter: they felt that she had single-handedly ruined Chandra's chance at family happiness. But equally, they admit that he had ruined her chance at the same.

Sumitra herself expressed no compunction; for it was she, and not Chandra, who had been wronged originally. She was the victim, not he. She talked to me candidly about an incident that I had heard from others: her first meeting with Tokiko in Nepal. Amanda had phoned her father one day, and a woman had answered the phone. When Amanda asked who she was, she answered, 'I'm Mrs Gurung.' Puzzled, Amanda hung up and told her mother what had happened. Sumitra phoned back and immediately realized it was Tokiko on the line.

She rushed over to Chandra's apartment, Amanda in tow. Tokiko and her younger son by Chandra, Eiki, were there. In Sumitra's version of events, they just met. In the version told by others, Sumitra created a scene.

I had also heard from others of an incident in which Sumitra's sister had set out to confront Tokiko in Japan when they both happened to be there. Sumitra had been intent on complicating Chandra and Tokiko's life together.

This—as it turned out—was unnecessary. Ultimately, Chandra and Tokiko both chose to live where they worked. Though married, they did not live together for more than brief spells while visiting each other. Chandra had no one in Nepal with whom he could share the minutiae of his days. To his closest confidants he sometimes expressed his loneliness, his despair. 'I seem to be unfortunate, Didi,' was what he told his sister Humkali.

Chandra was unfortunate, too, in that so much of the work he did at ACAP was undone after his departure from the trust. In losing him—and before him, Hemanta Mishra and Mingma Norbu Sherpa—the trust lost its credibility. In 1996, when the Maoists launched an armed insurgency—their 'People's

War'—ACAP came under renewed attack. With a reductive logic, the Maoists argued that because the trust was patronized by the royal family, all its projects, including ACAP, were royalist.

The trust had indeed deteriorated by then. When Gyanendra became king in 2001, he replaced King Birendra as the organization's patron. His son Crown Prince Paras—who had a history of drug abuse and manslaughter—became the chairman of the trust's board. In *Tiger Warden*, Laxmibadan Maskey recounts an incident that revealed how Prince Paras approached conservation:

> This incident is from when [my husband Tirtha Man Maskey] was the [director general of the Department of National Parks and Wildlife Conservation]; he went to Chitwan with His Highness Paras. This was before Paras's marriage. Paras was a hooligan from the start. Gyanendra had sent him to Chitwan under [my husband Tirtha Man Maskey's] charge. Oh…the trouble Paras sarkar created! There was a Vitara that had just come to the zoo, he drove it as though in the wind. Not a care where it might crash. He used to wake up for his morning breakfast at four in the afternoon. He used to eat his evening's dinner at two or three at night. No one ever knew when he'd get up. Everyone would feel harassed, just waiting and waiting. The week he stayed in Chitwan, he was no less than a wild animal himself. The week he stayed in Chitwan, he almost got beaten up after crashing into someone's car. After they found out he was the crown prince, they let him go. By the time he returned after a week in Chitwan, the zoo's new car was a wreck.

The zoo was under the management of the trust.

A March 2008 exposé in *Himal Khabarpatrika* revealed 'financial irregularity and administrative anarchy' in the trust. These included exorbitant hospitality and entertainment bills at board meetings and staff meetings; laptops and cars for the royal family; and expenses for the royal family's foreign excursions. A *Kantipur* report of October 2008 reported that these laptops and cars were never returned, not even after the monarchy was abolished earlier that year. 'What is more surprising is that the Office of the Auditor-General, which is responsible for auditing all the public accounts throughout the country, has "overlooked" financial irregularities of this extent,' the March 2008 exposé claimed, going on to conclude: 'it is evident…that the royal family and the Trust authorities and personnel have been using the Trust as a milking cow'.

Such behaviour made King Gyanendra and Crown Prince Paras increasingly unpopular, and strengthened the Maoists' call for republicanism. When the trust helped to organize the government's gift of rhinoceroses to zoos in San Francisco, Washington DC, and Vienna, it was easy for the Maoists to spread the accusation that the organization was trafficking in endangered species. In the villages, the Maoists accused the ACAP staff of smuggling wildlife contraband. As criticism of the trust mounted, the trust's chapters in the United Kingdom, the United States, Canada, France, the Netherlands, Germany and Japan began to question the organization's direction. Funding dwindled. Morale was low.

During the Maoist insurgency—and the military counter-insurgency—the field staff of non-government organizations found themselves caught in the crossfire. The Maoists began to attack ACAP's field offices in 2001. The first attack, on the office in Lwang, was comparatively mild. The Maoists warned the staff beforehand and even allowed them to leave the building. No one was hurt, but all the paperwork was burned and the computers destroyed. The Maoists left after painting slogans against Gyanendra and Paras on the walls.

That office was eventually bombed again, leaving it in ruins. The Bhujung office was attacked, and all the papers were destroyed. The office in Siklis was forced to shut. The Maoists forced donations from ACAP's field staff, stopped staff movement, and threatened villagers against working on ACAP's projects. They brought most of the field offices to a standstill. (Only the offices in Mustang and Manang Districts remained unaffected.) There was no convincing the Maoists that ACAP was not, in their terms, royalist. There was no convincing them that they were not being radical, but destructive.

In Ghandruk in 2004, the Maoists turned to murder. Siddhartha Bajra Bajracharya had been in Ghandruk just a month earlier. Gehendra Gurung was heading ACAP's office there at the time. The staff had been facing threats from the Maoists; but they were still negotiating some space to work. 'The night guard used to lock you into the office building at night,' Siddhartha told me, recalling the discomfiting atmosphere at the time of his visit. 'I could use the space inside the building, but I didn't feel safe. I kept thinking—what happens if the Maoists attack? How will I get out?'

His worst fears came to pass a month later. The Maoists had just staged a military attack on the Royal Nepal Army base in neighbouring Myagdi District. The army retaliated swiftly: patrols chased after the Maoists, hunting them from village to village, and killing them where they found them. Fleeing, many of the Maoists came to shelter in Ghandruk. As Siddhartha recounted the story to me: 'Someone from Ghandruk apparently informed the army about this. So the army came to Ghandruk, went from home to home, took some Maoists out to the helipad'—near the ACAP office building—'and shot them dead. So the Maoists had a retaliatory killing.'

Ishwor Gurung, a Ghandruk native, ran a telephone booth from where the Maoists believed the army had been tipped off. The Maoists killed him. The same night, they killed one of the three main leaders of the village, Dilman Gurung. Dilman Gurung had chaired ACAP's tourism committee, which set the rules regarding campgrounds, restaurants and lodges. He had also been a member of the conservation committee. He usually lived in Pokhara, and was just visiting Ghandruk at the time. The Maoists believed he had told the army of their whereabouts.

They killed him in the most chilling way. 'They took him out to the edge of the cliff'—the cliff on which the ACAP office building stood—'and tortured him,' Siddhartha said to me. 'Everything could be heard throughout the village. After they killed him, the Maoists threatened the rest of the villagers—this can happen to you too.' Finally, they bombed the office building—the building that had once housed ACAP's headquarters—demolishing it entirely.

The Maoists might have also killed a third person, an ACAP staff, had she been in the village that night. Jagan Subba Gurung, a Ghandruk local, had started off at ACAP in women's development, but over the years had developed an interest in hotel management, and opened a lodge in Ghandruk, which she described to me as a 'model guest house'. She explained, 'I wanted to have organic vegetables, and set an example for how to run an environmentally friendly hotel.' The Maoists believed that she too had informed on them to the army. 'I wasn't even there at the time, but that's what they believed,' she told me. As punishment, they came twice to her lodge, and, at gunpoint, robbed her once of money, and another time of fifty to sixty tolas (about 500-600 grams) of gold.

Fearing for her life, she relocated to Pokhara. Gehendra Gurung eventually resigned from ACAP. The rest of the ACAP staff were moved to the Pokhara office, or—as there was little work to do—let go.

With the murder of Dilman Gurung, all three village leaders that Chandra had cultivated at ACAP's inception were gone. The village mukhiya, Min Bahadur Gurung, had succumbed to liver failure some years before. Tek Bahadur Gurung had moved to Pokhara during the war and had died in a freak accident, crushed in the collapse of a hospital building. 'All three original conservation leaders were gone,' Siddhartha said.

And the dynamics of the village were utterly changed by now. The war had polarized the villagers and exposed rifts in the village society. As Shailendra Thakali put it to me, wistfully: 'A village just can't be a village…' Then he admitted that, yes, there had been a certain conservatism in the way ACAP used to work, seeking the cooperation of traditional leaders, and inevitably bolstering their status. But ACAP's mandate had been to give the local people control over their natural resources. It had not been its mandate to also rid the villages of conservatism. But for the Maoists, of course, nothing less than revolution would do.

In Siklis, the Maoists took over the lands of the village development committee's chairman, prompting him to move to Pokhara for fear of his life. Then they turned to Chandra and his family. Though Ratansingh had not ruled in the manner of the mukhiyas of yore, those who resented him—and which village would not have its rifts and rivalries?—found allies in the Maoists. 'There was an undertone of sixteen-jaat and four-jaat rivalry in the village,' Ghana explained to me. Those of the sixteen 'lesser' Gurung clans harboured some resentment against the four 'higher' clans. (Indeed, Harka Gurung, from a sixteen-jaat clan, mercilessly ribbed Chandra about his privileged birth.) Ratansingh and Krishnakumari were of the 'high' Gothane clan. They were, in the Maoists' view, class enemies: reactionaries, feudals.

In Pokhara, I learned of the darkest aspect of the Maoists' campaign against Chandra. Chandra's nephew Krishnaman Gurung had been on the way to his father's village, Khilang, in the spring of 2006 when he heard that the Maoists had posted a public letter to Chandra. This, while Siklis was under Maoist occupation, and when many of the Maoists' senior leaders—Pushpa Kamal Dahal 'Prachanda' and Baburam Bhattarai—were living there.

'I heard they had posted the letter in a place called Jyaundo,' Krishnaman recalled to me. 'So I went there, and found it pasted on to a board.' The letter accused Chandra of being an informant. Krishnaman was unable to tear the letter off the board—it would rip—so he copied it, word for word, recalling: 'It said that he was occupying a high post at the King Mahendra Trust, and had taken part in a demonstration against the democratic movement. It said he raised money to suppress the democratic movement, and he sent venison and herbs to the royal palace.' The letter demanded that Chandra come to Siklis within fifteen days to defend himself, or else face 'physical action'. In the Maoists' lexicon, this could range from toiling in a labour camp to torture and murder.

The charges were ridiculous, not least because Chandra was long gone from the trust. He had already joined WWF Nepal by then. Yet these charges could not be ignored, for the Maoists had proven themselves capable of savagery against those they deemed to be enemies. For as long as the Maoists occupied Siklis, Chandra would be unsafe returning there.

Chandra happened to be abroad when the letter was posted. 'We knew he would call when he got back,' Krishnaman said, referring to his uncle's habit of telephoning his mother—Humkali—immediately on landing at the airport. 'We didn't know how to tell him about the letter,' Krishnaman told me. 'My mother just kept crying.'

When they did give Chandra the news, he asked Krishnaman to fax him the letter. 'He said—I'll go to the office and stay by the fax machine, send it at once.' Krishnaman did so, and waited for a response. 'Fifteen days passed, then twenty. We were very worried,' he told me. At the time, the top Maoist leaders had left Siklis. There was no one in authority to reason with. Krishnaman told me that some of the villagers came to Pokhara to defend Chandra before the leaders of the Maoists' Gurung wing, the Tamu Mukti Morcha. They even met the

Maoists' politburo member Dev Gurung. 'They said, in front of Dev Gurung, that they were willing to spill blood over this matter,' Krishnaman told me. 'Later, when Prachanda and Baburam returned to the village, they talked to them too.' It was only after this that the Maoists' local secretary in Siklis, who went by the nom de guerre 'Karan', withdrew the charges against Chandra. 'He admitted that there was no basis for them, he said they had made a mistake,' Krishnaman said hotly. Then he fell silent. And in that silence I ruminated over the difficulty of doing constructive work in Nepal. That someone as can-do as Chandra could be targeted as an enemy, that all his work could be undone, that so many of ACAP's gains could be destroyed…to clear the way for what Maoist utopia? Need we wipe out all that has come before, to start anew? Is this what Nepal was going to have to do now?

For everyone who had worked at ACAP in its heyday, the questions—the 'what ifs'—were unavoidable later on. Would ACAP have survived the Maoists' onslaughts had Chandra remained in the trust? Had Prince Gyanendra not tossed him aside? Had the ACAP staff paid more attention to the administration side of work? Had the organization's vision been less moderate, and more revolutionary? Yet the organization's vision had been revolutionary: to have local people manage their own resources. Had this not been revolutionary enough?

Dibya Gurung told me of a recent visit that she had taken to Ghandruk. She had not been there for many years; and now she found the village quite changed. 'It's all divide-and-rule now,' she said wistfully. 'The charge that ACAP was feudalistic...' she sighed. 'I suppose society's attitudes have changed so fast. Who could have foreseen that?' She and I laughed about the way the female staff used to wear traditional clothes, so as to fit in. 'Now, all the village girls are wearing pants,' she said. Then she grew thoughtful. 'Sometimes I do wonder whether we did the right thing. I mean, we did empower the local people,' she said, 'but it was all so—ad hoc.'

Others shared these mixed feelings. Talking on Skype from Australia, Hum Bahadur Gurung mentioned the lack of clarity regarding the community forest users groups' mandate: 'The committees couldn't punish any wrongdoing, they didn't have any legal authority,' he said. This was what he felt when focusing narrowly on conservation. But like Dibya, he could not help but ruminate on the larger changes, and the radical consciousness brought about by the Maoists. 'Of course the marginalized didn't benefit as much,' he said. 'The smart people of the village would sit in on all the committees, and, well, they would pass decisions that benefited themselves. The feudal system can't be changed overnight,' he said. 'It does need to be changed. The Maoists, with their demand for a federal system, for greater local authority, for transparency—that's all good,' he said. 'But we can't just let go of everything. There were some good things there, you know.'

This regret was mirrored by the people of the area. In Siklis I had spoken, one evening, to the local schoolteacher Suresh Gurung, known locally as Suresh Sir. We had met in Chandra's family home as a local mothers' group sat by, commiserating with Sumitra and Amanda Manandhar Gurung. Having observed ACAP's work from its inception in 1990, Suresh Sir was able to give me a thoughtful, balanced view on its dramatic rise, as well as its paltry demise.

He felt that Chandra's roots—his intimate knowledge of village life—had been the key to ACAP's success. 'Many people who reach high positions, they don't have any experience of village life,' he said. 'They might have lived in the city, or even abroad—but if they've experienced the village in their childhood, that's better.' Chandra had done that. 'ACAP benefited from that, it was able to take advantage of that.'

Nevertheless, he felt that the organization's work had remained incomplete. 'If this had been like other places, it might have changed more,' he said. 'You think it's a Gurung village, so everyone gets along; but there are certain…problems, within.' He grew vague about the problems, telling me only that some people had opposed the organization. Chandra had wanted to do much more in Siklis, he said. 'But some people said yes, and some people said no. We Gurungs,' he said, only half in jest, 'we may seem simple, but we're actually quite clever. If we see some benefit, we'll go along with things; otherwise we'll act stubborn. We won't argue, the way others do. We just won't do what we're supposed to.'

It was not true, he said, that ACAP had done nothing to change society. 'The work wasn't finished—it had to end before it could finish,' he said. He felt something new should be started now; the organization should resume its work. 'Some things did happen.' He paused a while, considering. 'Some things seemed to happen, but then…' He chose his words carefully. 'Emptiness descended. Something was just about to happen, and then…' Again, he paused. 'That's why, now, the village feels unchanged, that's why it feels just as it used to be.'

In Pokhara, Lal Prasad Gurung—who was heading ACAP—assured me that the organization would continue, if in an altered state. After the Maoists entered the peace process, they said that ACAP's staff could return to the village. 'It was the local community who did the work anyway,' Lal Prasad pointed out to me. 'Look, I'm from that area too. We're not talking about outsiders here.' By this time, the trust's name had already been changed to the National Trust for Nature Conservation. The prime minister had replaced the king as the patron; and the minister of forestry and soil conservation had replaced the crown prince as the chairman of the board. (To boot, the minister at the time was a Maoist, Matrika Yadav.) An experienced environmentalist—Siddhartha Bajra Bajracharya—was now heading the trust. Nevertheless, there were moves to make ACAP independent of the trust. ACAP would, in the future, be accountable to a Pokhara-based council, Lal Prasad told me. He was cautiously optimistic about the future of the organization. 'We're planning to take back the field offices soon,' he said. 'The Maoists are telling us to come back to the villages. They just want the budget to be transparent,' he said. 'They want the local people to get jobs. That's what we want too,' he said. 'That's exactly what we want.'

VINDICATION

ACAP's demise might have plunged Chandra into despair had he not found his professional footing again, at WWF Nepal. He came to head WWF Nepal in 1999, after Mingma Norbu Sherpa left to join WWF US. Mingma recommended Chandra as his replacement. The decision had not been without qualms. Though the two were close, there was a serious divergence in their styles. Whereas Mingma liked to work quietly, out of the limelight, Chandra courted publicity for every achievement. Whereas Mingma was methodical, the spontaneous Chandra could be disorganized. Those who were privy to internal discussions told me that Mingma was not sure that Chandra should replace him. Chandra had, after all, no background in the natural sciences; and there were other experts, such as Dr Pralad Yonzon, or even WWF's Ukesh Bhuju, who were as qualified for the job. But in the end Mingma recommended Chandra as his replacement, once again vacating his post for him, as he had at ACAP.

The careers of many of ACAP's staff were intertwined with theirs: over the years they drifted over to WWF, hired either by Mingma or by Chandra. Tshering Lama, who had worked at ACAP, had been with WWF a year already when Chandra took over from Mingma. Talking to me over the telephone from China, where she was working on a project on Asian big cats, Tshering said of Chandra, 'This was when he came into his own.'

Chandra was, as ever, driven to do everything properly. He arrived early, by 8.00 in the morning, and left late, at 6.30 p.m.—unusually long hours in lackadaisical Kathmandu. As at ACAP, he expected the staff to do the same. 'He was overworking us again,' Ghana Shyam Gurung (Ghurmet) said. 'Maybe because he had no family at home—there was no Saturday, no Sunday for him.' Tshering added, 'He saw that we were getting burned out. He realized he had done that to us at ACAP too. He eased up after that.'

Unlike at ACAP and the trust, at WWF, Chandra did not focus on work in the field. He applied himself instead to organization-building. Anil Manandhar, who had left ACAP for a consultancy on the parks-vs-people conflict at UNDP, and then joined WWF, told me that Mingma's work at WWF had set the stage for Chandra. 'There was a good management team in place when he joined.' This ensured that the administrative weaknesses that had plagued Chandra earlier were no longer an issue. He was free, here, to concentrate on his strengths: public relations and fundraising.

The organization burgeoned under his leadership. In 1996, Mingma Sherpa had begun a community agro-forestry project in the Sagarmatha National Park and its buffer zone. WWF had also launched a Northern Mountains Conservation Project the same year in the remote western districts of Mugu and Dolpo. The organization's development, research and monitoring programmes, and communication and conservation education programmes were ongoing.

Chandra set about securing new projects—large, ambitious

projects with large budgets and ample funds. One of these was the Kangchanjunga Conservation Area Project. KCAP had only just been conceptualized when Mingma left. Upon joining WWF, Chandra launched a massive public relations campaign to secure the project for WWF. For this, he competed directly against the trust, which also wanted KCAP for itself. By this time Jaya Pratap Rana had left the trust, and Arup Rajouria, who had earlier worked under Chandra, had come to head the organization. Chandra could not brook Arup Rajouria, whom he viewed as a palace insider. He did not bother to disguise his dislike. Relations between WWF and the trust chilled to the point where the heads of these, the country's two major conservation organizations, were not on talking terms. 'He took it a little too far,' Siddhartha Bajra Bajracharya told me, laughing. 'He wouldn't even talk to me any more, he'd say that anything he said to me, I'd pass on to Arup.'

To secure KCAP, WWF had to get the government behind WWF. In a country lacking set procedures for policymaking, he turned for help to Harka Gurung and Tirtha Man Maskey, both of whom knew their way around the bureaucracy. Then Chandra focused all his powers of persuasion on lobbying. 'He could work out all the details with the government, from the secretary level to the ministry level,' Ghana told me. Anil Manandhar commented on his excellent rapport with key officials: 'He was very close to Rabi Bista, who used to be the secretary. He was the one who convinced the government to pass the Tarai Arc project. And he was close to Jamuna Krishna Tamrakar, the chief coordinator. Dibya Dev Bhatta, too—the director general of the Department of Forests.' As

Anil explained, the regulations about conservation areas were as yet unclear: 'The legal part was still to be worked out. The Department of National Parks and Wildlife Conservation was making regulations—for ACAP, KCAP.' Even as this legislation was being drafted, Chandra succeeded in securing KCAP for WWF.

This was a major success for WWF, and, for Chandra, a personal vindication: for KCAP was but a logical extension of ACAP. While ACAP had promoted community-managed conservation, KCAP took things a step further, to launch community-owned conservation. The local people would be granted ownership of their own resources for the first time in the country's history. Through WWF he could pursue the mission he had launched at ACAP: promoting local autonomy over natural resources. Later, when WWF launched even more ambitious projects—such as the Tarai Arc Landscape, or the Sacred Himalayan Landscape—Chandra had less attention to pay to KCAP. But, as Sarala Khaling of WWF put it, 'KCAP was huge at the start. It meant everything to him.'

Chandra's other major responsibility at WWF was to obtain funds. As at the trust, he worked with Mingma Norbu Sherpa on this: from Nepal, Chandra would pitch programmes, and Mingma, in the United States, would find international support for them. As before, the partnership proved extremely effective.

Chandra brought to WWF the same great, good luck—the charmed quality—he had earlier brought to ACAP. Mostly, this was the product of his work ethic. Tshering Lama told me about the relentlessness with which he pursued the Tarai Arc Landscape project—WWF's largest project to date.

The Tarai Arc Landscape was part of a global WWF initiative to construct wildlife corridors to link fragmented ecological 'islands' so as to create more viable habitats for wildlife. This had become the focus of conservation worldwide around the turn of the millennium. In Nepal, the 'landscape' approach marked a whole new stage. Conservation work had started with saving one or two species, and had progressed to establishing national parks, then conservation areas. Now it was set to view conservation more holistically as a matter of ecologically sound landscaping.

Not all donors who were willing to fund the Tarai Arc Landscape felt that WWF was the right organization to manage it. 'There was some opposition from DFID,' Tshering explained. This British aid organization felt that though WWF might know about community forestry, it did not know how to implement community development work—a key part of the project. But Chandra's formal training had been in participatory development. 'He went on a massive campaign,' Tshering recalled. 'He'd call up people and ask for meetings, and we'd go and give presentations. After a couple of months, we'd do it all over again.' She laughed. 'He basically battered the donors into dialogue.'

Winning the Tarai Arc Landscape was another major boost for WWF.

Chandra worked at a furious pace to get all this done. 'He spent half his time abroad,' said Bandana Yonzon Lepcha, who for some years worked as his assistant. WWF held several annual meetings that Chandra had to attend; he also had to attend other international meetings. 'He was always going out,' Jit Bahadur Sunuwar, WWF's office helper, told me, 'Japan, Germany, UK.' His nephew Major Hitman Gurung, talking to me at the Waterloo station in London, said how his uncle would storm into town, and immediately start meeting friends. 'He never wanted to just sit still,' he said. 'No matter where his friends were, he'd seek them out. Even his old friends—he'd seek them out, wherever they were. And these weren't just ordinary people,' he laughed. 'He'd meet Field Marshal John Chapman, General Sir Sam Cowan. He came to attend Lord Camoy's son's wedding.' But Chandra was just as much at ease with the 'small people', he said. 'He'd come, and he'd say, let's go, come, come, let's go and meet so-and-so. For me, when he came, it was always a whirl.'

In Nepal, too, Chandra networked tirelessly. To the surprise of those whom he came to consider his 'core group'—the staff he had mentored at ACAP—he befriended even those who had earlier harmed him: the trust staff who had leaked documents to the media, the journalists who had cast aspersions about corruption at ACAP. Chandra did not just befriend these 'foes'; he actually won them over as avid supporters. Even more surprisingly, he returned to boosting Prince Gyanendra. I, who was not in daily contact with him when he joined WWF, learned of his return to form from the headline news of a gala that WWF hosted in 2000, a gala attended by Prince Philip, WWF International's president emeritus. The gala celebrated the offering of twenty-six 'sacred gifts for a living planet'—the kind of warm-and-fuzzy celebration that Chandra loved to organize. Chandra had Prince Gyanendra give a keynote address on the occasion. Why aid a man who had, in Chandra's own words, tossed him away like a fly?

There is, at the heart of every person, an enigma, and Chandra's enigma was to seek entry into the Kathmandu establishment, an establishment that was reluctant to admit outsiders like him. If he bore any resentment against Prince Gyanendra, or against those who had once set out to harm him, it did not show. This puzzled everyone to whom I spoke.

'He was a man with a big heart,' was how WWF's driver, Hira Kaji Shrestha, explained it. He and WWF's office helper Jit Bahadur Sunuwar saw more of Chandra's personal life than most WWF staff. Jit Bahadur even stayed over at Chandra's house at one point. He told me that at the end of his life Chandra had grown very close to Harka Gurung—whom Chandra referred to as Harka-dai, as an elder brother—and to Tirtha Man Maskey. 'He was also close to the ambassador from Finland, Pauli,' Jit Bahadur told me. 'That ambassador got him the medal from Finland.' This was Finland's Knight First Class, Order of the Lion, which Chandra won in 2004. 'He was good friends with other ambassadors too, even the previous ones—the US, UK ambassadors. His relations with diplomats were excellent.'

He always followed the latest news, and made sure that the WWF staff did too, berating them if they were not up on current events. 'He was always reading one book or another,' WWF's Sarala Khaling told me. 'They'd be books that everyone was reading, like *The Da Vinci Code*, or Bill Clinton's memoirs.' It was important to him, she said, to keep up with cocktail-party chatter.

An outsider—a boy from Siklis—Chandra was determined, at WWF, to break into Kathmandu society for good. He attended soirées almost every evening. 'He never said no to invitations,' reported Prajana Waiba Pradhan, his last assistant at WWF. Hira Kaji Shrestha told me, 'When there weren't foreign guests at home, he'd have Jar-sah'bs, Kar-sah'bs, the police bosses.' He named the generals and colonels and police chiefs that Chandra was close to: all janajatis, outsiders to the Kathmandu establishment. Hira Kaji said, 'They'd sing dohori songs'—duets of the kind that are sung in the Annapurna area—'till late into the night. They'd bring singers to the house. They'd have beer, they'd eat meat. It was always,' he added, using the English term, 'very romantic.'

As he settled into his work at WWF, Chandra even took up golf, often reaching the army golf course at six in the morning. (My mother, an avid golfer, often saw him there. She said he would bring food for a dog that lived on the course.) On weekends Chandra would play at the course in Gokarna, where Kathmandu's elite congregated. His game was not good. 'I swear he took up golf just to be able to hobnob with diplomats,' several people said to me, laughing. 'I don't think he enjoyed the game, he just saw it as socially advantageous.' But as Anil Manandhar put it, 'All the parties he went to, all the socializing he did—it was all meant to help the organization.'

He remained, till the end, a micromanager. 'He had an eye for detail,' Sarala Khaling told me. 'He would check commas, decimals, capitals—everything had to be just right.' His temper was notorious in the office. 'You could see him getting angry, his face would darken. Then he would start shouting, without even asking about anything. Lots of the staff were scared of him,' she chuckled. 'He'd get upset over the smallest things—

if the dais wasn't placed properly, if the names weren't in order, if a meeting fell through, if someone didn't address a minister properly. He couldn't hide what was inside. He would just start to shout.'

Bandana Yonzon Lepcha quoted him: 'He'd shout, "Ke re?" when he was mad.' Ke re: what's that? His other favourite word was, in English, 'Horrible!' 'He'd also say "Raddi!"' She repeated the word, which means nonsense: 'Raddi!'

Prajana Waiba Pradhan said the staff would give him a wide berth when they saw he was angry. Afterwards, he would come around and apologize. 'He always said sorry.'

Remembering how attractive a figure he had cut at ACAP, I asked her, and several others of the female staff at WWF, whether they hadn't had a crush on him, if only in secret. They invariably looked aghast. Finally, Sarala said to me, 'He was a bit old.'

Indeed, he would have been different from how I remembered him. He was fifty-six when he died. The younger staff at WWF even saw him as quaintly out of date. Bandana told me, 'People would tease him, like he was a granddad, because he'd say things like, "A virus came and sat in my computer."' Prajana agreed: 'He was always saying, email should be banned. And he was terrified of viruses.' Mistaking a pop-up for a virus, he once telephoned the Internet server for help, she told me. Another time, he was having trouble with a new telephone, a Motorola. 'The battery was low,' she recalled. 'He said, "There's a virus in my mobile phone."'

Still, he kept abreast of everything that was going on at the office. Ghana told me, 'He was a hands-on boss. There was no chain of command. He was the boss of everything.' But

Chandra was nowhere as pell-mell as he had been at ACAP. 'He was only about twelve per cent chaotic. For the most part, he was okay here.'

Earlier, Chandra had brought ACAP, and the trust, unprecedented prestige. Now he brought WWF to a new height. The Tarai Arc Landscape project, launched in 2001, focused on more than half the southern lowlands—west from the Parsa Wildlife Reserve, all through the tarai, to the Shuklaphanta Wildlife Reserve on the western border with India. (It also extended into India.) In 2003, WWF launched the Climate Change programme, following this with the Freshwater programme in 2005, and the Sustainable Livelihoods programme in 2006. In 2006, WWF launched the evocatively named Sacred Himalayan Landscape programme, a project involving Nepal, India and Bhutan that focused, in Nepal, east from the Langtang National Park all the way to the border with India. WWF reached its highest level of funding under Chandra. Work was proceeding at a phenomenal rate. Morale was extremely high.

To me, all this recalled ACAP. Less familiar were Chandra's attempts to boost teamwork at WWF, attempts that seemed—to me—to come from office-management manuals. But Tshering Lama insisted, 'The way he got the whole WWF team to come together and work—it was amazing. He really knew how to get the best out of people.' Chandra set up prizes for grassroots conservationists. He also invented prizes for the neatest office: the prize was a broom-and-pan set. At annual office meetings, there would be games between two in-house teams, the Orange Piranhas (the team that Chandra was in) and the Mighty Unicorns. Invariably, there would be singing and dancing as well. Sarala Khaling commented, 'He was always saying, "This is what we did at ACAP."' Those words were always on his lips.' The lusty lament 'Sohra barsa umeramaa' remained his favourite song all his life.

What Chandra did above all, noted Tshering, was to invest in the staff. 'He pushed us to develop ourselves,' she told me. He never begrudged the staff any opportunities, sending them off for training, trotting them along to meetings, exposing them to professional challenges. He sent Tshering on a management course to the Philippines. And when Yeshi Choden Lama was deferring her master's in science, he insisted that she do it. 'He always said, "Staff are my greatest resources,"' recalled Bandana Yonzon Lepcha. Talking about Chandra at ACAP and the trust, Hum Bahadur Gurung had noted that everyone who had encountered Chandra had benefited personally. About Chandra at WWF, Tshering agreed, 'He helped to develop everyone.'

The organization was not without challenges, of course. The country was at war. Work in the field was affected, sometimes badly. The war significantly delayed KCAP's launch, and its structure had to be changed: 'Instead of being village based, it had to be district based,' Ghana told me. 'The Lelep and Ghunsa offices moved to Taplejung bazaar. Dawa Tshering Sherpa—who also died in the helicopter crash—helped negotiate a lot of these things.'

In the war-torn tarai as well, the organization had difficulty implementing work. The state was weak, and there were constant blockades on the highways and closures in the towns. The Maoists had a strong presence in many of the villages; and—as had happened in Ghandruk—they often attacked the state security forces, who then retaliated. The field staff had to watch out for themselves. They also had to be on good terms with both sides, to be able to work at all. Neutrality was key to survival.

Several of WWF's staff recalled a field trip that Chandra took, in which he met the Maoists by chance. 'This was on a trip from Chitwan to the west, all the way to Shuklaphanta,' said Hira Kaji Shrestha, who drove one of the cars on that trip. 'It was during the ceasefire right after the Armed Police chief, Krishna Mohan Shrestha, was killed.' This was in January 2003. Hira Kaji said that 'all the big bosses' were along for the trip: the heads of the Netherlands Development Organisation and the UN Development Programme, the director general of the Department of Forests. 'There were four cars!' The District Forest Officer was also along for the trip.

As Dhan Rai of WWF told me, when they reached Kailali, in a section called the Basanta Corridor, they heard a rumour that the Maoists had been felling trees illegally. 'They wanted to see if it was true,' Dhan said. They drove five kilometres into the forest to investigate. There they reached a Maoist camp. Their convoy was quickly surrounded by rebels, 300 or 400 in all. Everyone got out. Unwisely, the District Forest Officer began to lecture the Maoists about the illegality of felling trees. He was quickly surrounded by hostile rebels. The others took in the sight of the camp. Some began to take pictures. 'The Maoists blew a whistle, they forbade them to take pictures,' recalled Hira Kaji. 'They confiscated the chips from all the cameras.' All misunderstandings were cleared eventually. Their leaders explained that they were being especially vigilant because of a recent ambush by the army. They said they had the permission of the Village People's Committee—a parallel Maoist local government body—to cut trees. 'But otherwise they were civil,' said Hira Kaji. 'They spoke politely, and returned the chips at the end. They even staged "revolutionary" songs and dances to welcome their visitors,' he said. When they saw them off, they directed them out of the forest. 'We left by another road.'

For Chandra, this meeting would have been interesting, if not entirely convincing. The Maoists had all but undone ACAP; Chandra had himself come in their crosshairs in Siklis. And just as the Maoists viewed environmentalists with mistrust, as being royalists, environmentalists were wary of the Maoists. After 1990, it had taken much effort for environmentalists to get the democratic political parties to support conservation; when caught, many poachers and wildlife contraband smugglers used to turn to party leaders for protection. (They still do.) There was some question (there still is) about whether the Maoists would be just another source of such protection for a whole new set of poachers and smugglers. Yet it was also tactically important for environmentalists to forge an understanding with all political players, to remain neutral. Politically, Chandra was mixed—a promoter of local autonomy, a liberal, a visionary, the son of a mukhiya. He did not favour one political party over the others, but the misunderstandings between him and the then-underground Maoists would have been too big to overcome just yet. That rapprochement was a few years off. At the time, no one could have guessed that just three years later, in the year of Chandra's death, the Maoists would be in government.

Chandra's work at WWF did not take him to the field often; but when he did get out, he fit right in, as he had in his ACAP days. Tilak Dhakal, a WWF staff at the Tarai Arc Landscape project, remarked, 'When he was with villagers, he behaved like them, like a local farmer. But when he was with the ministers, he behaved like a minister.'

Chandra's field trips were always adventurous, and sometimes risky. His can-do attitude—bhaihaalchha: of course it'll happen—made him overconfident at times. Dhan Rai, who used to work in WWF's Northern Mountains Conservation Project, told me of a trip Chandra took to Dolpo with a group of colleagues and donors. The group consisted of the head of USAID, Joanne Hale, along with another USAID colleague, whose name Dhan could not remember, but whom he described as a man of few words. Harka Gurung, Tirtha Man Maskey and Chandra's close friend and physician, Dr Buddha Basnet, were also along. 'He always travelled like that, with donors and experts and friends—in a big group,' Dhan said. The trip coincided with a once-in-every-twelve-years festival at the Shey Gompa, a monastery in northern Dolpo.

The group flew in from Kathmandu in a helicopter, and was dropped off near the Shey monastery. The festival lasted three days. But by then the sky had so clouded over that the helicopter could not return to pick them up.

They stayed in their tents on the monastery grounds and

waited. 'Everyone who had come to the festival had left,' Dhan said. 'There was no village near the monastery. It was difficult to find even food. There was just one woman who stayed at the gompa, the caretaker. It was just her and us.' With some effort, he bought some potatoes and meat from passing yak herders. Dhan said, 'The helicopter pilot was Gunjaman Lama'—a good friend of Chandra, one of the janajati army officers with whom he socialized—'and every morning, we would wait for the helicopter to come, and every morning, it wouldn't show up.' He laughed. 'We waited eight days!'

It was cold in the high-altitude air; the facilities were very rudimentary. Yet everyone was stoic. Buddha Basnet, who also told me about the incident, recalled that Harka Gurung had brought along notes he had written from decades ago, when he had first visited the region: 'He was comparing the place as it was then to how he found it now.' Claiming that he would suffer high-altitude sickness if he could not drink, Harka Gurung made sure there was some local brew at hand. Everyone swapped stories to pass the time. After a few days Chandra borrowed playing cards from the porters; and he, Harka Gurung, Tirtha Man Maskey and Buddha Basnet whiled away the days playing cards. Joanna Hale would walk around the monastery, Dhan said, but carefully, for she had had her kneecaps replaced, and the ground was slippery from the rain. The other USAID official read constantly: 'He only had one book, but he read and re-read it, as though trying to memorize it!'

Eventually, Tirtha Man Maskey ran out of his high blood pressure pills. Something had to be done. The nearest airport at the district headquarters, Dunai, was more than a week's walk away. There was no option but to try to get there.

'We left behind one person'—a porter—'and headed downhill,' Dhan recalled. He had found a few yaks on hire. The group tied their bags on to the backs of these beasts, and set off with the yak herder leading the way. Several hours on, though, they heard the sound of a helicopter overhead. It was their long-delayed pick-up. 'We all waved madly' said Dhan, 'we were worried the pilot wouldn't see us. We all waved to get his attention.' The pilot spotted them, and landed in a nearby clearing, setting the yaks in a panic with the noise. Dhan laughed. 'The yaks went completely wild—they ran straight up a cliff, with all the bags still on their backs! We had to chase them, and bring them back, and unload all the bags.' In the confusion, he put his own bags on to the helicopter, though he was staying behind. 'When the helicopter took off, I realized I didn't have a single change of clothes left!'

For everyone on the trip, professionals with hectic schedules, the delay must have been extremely inconvenient. Chandra's confidence—bhaihaalchha: of course it'll happen—had bordered on overconfidence. In retrospect, the trip was also quite risky. As Buddha Basnet put it, 'After we boarded the helicopter, the pilot pulled out a topographical map and began to check it against the view out the cockpit window. I asked, "Why do you need to do that? Don't you have a radar to guide you?" And he said, "No, this is how you fly helicopters." That was when I realized that helicopter pilots need to be able to see everything clearly, they can't fly through clouds, the way planes can. I didn't know that till then,' he said.

A HOUSE IN KATHMANDU

By then Chandra had taken so many helicopter trips that he was, it seems, unafraid of travelling in any condition. Or he felt protected. He was not so much religious as superstitious, consulting astrologers at important life junctures, and turning to his soaltee Professor Jagman Gurung to help negotiate the world of spirits. Shortly after joining WWF, he had his soaltee perform a puja, a prayer, in the office. 'He was modern, of course, but he was also grounded in his culture,' Tshering Lama explained. 'He was cosmopolitan, but really, also—he just did whatever he pleased.' Chandra felt that there were 'bad vibes' in the WWF office. His soaltee performed the puja over a weekend, when the office was empty. 'There are nails driven into the door—you can still see them there. At the front entrance.' This assured him that the office was clear of malign spirits, Tshering told me. Then she segued into a thought: 'You know, maybe his new house wasn't so lucky for him.'

Just a few years before his death, Chandra had finally given in to the Nepali dream, to have a house in Kathmandu. Upon joining WWF, he had begun to earn well for the first time in his life. His plan, as he told his core group, was to remain with WWF for several more years, to see his son Adhish through college. Then he would retire and 'do something small'. The house was part of his retirement plan. He wanted to grow old here, in style.

In proper style. Before selecting the property in Dhapasi, on a hill turned away from the urban sprawl of Kathmandu, Chandra looked at plots all over the city, following the advice of friends and family. He even bought a plot in the upscale neighbourhood of Budhanilkantha, but—wanting to live near his own people—he sold it eventually. The plot in Dhapasi was close to the house of one of his core group members, Shailendra Thakali. It stood in a large, as-yet undeveloped gated community on the edge of a hill, with a view on to the rim of Kathmandu valley. Chandra persuaded his nephew in the British Gurkhas, Major Hitman Gurung, to buy an adjacent plot. Hitman's brother Krishnaman told me that Chandra wanted the family to remain close: 'He wanted our family to set an example. He wanted all six of my brothers to live in one place.' This, he admitted, was unrealistic—it had taken the brothers seventeen years to even have a reunion, just a year before Chandra's death.

The house was Chandra's dream home. 'He spent so much money on it, oh god,' Tshering told me, groaning at the memory. 'He was constantly redoing it!' Earlier, Chandra had designed ACAP's headquarters in Ghandruk to be modern in its use of space, yet traditional in its use of materials and design elements. Now he designed his own house with the same modern spaces, and the same mix of Newari and Gurung design elements. His wife Tokiko was involved in the house designing. It had five bedrooms, an airy study and spacious rooms for entertaining. With a stupa up front, the house had an elegant air. Chandra went into debt in its making, complained Hira Kaji Shrestha. 'He got swindled on the architecture!' Construction was also delayed because he had to keep travelling for work. His soaltee Hum Bahadur Gurung finally helped to supervise the builders.

Chandra also overspent on furnishing the house. 'He had high taste,' said Bandana Yonzon Lepcha, who, along with others at WWF, took Chandra shopping. 'He liked modern furniture, IKEA-style furniture.' 'He always listened too much to the ladies,' was Hira Kaji's opinion. 'He bought all this furniture—then found out it was all fake. He sent it all to his sister in Pokhara. Everything. Then he bought genuine furniture at Alternative Furniture.' He clucked. 'The money he spent!' Everything in the house had to be just so. Chandra was a social drinker, moderate; but he so loved to entertain that he made sure to have a full bar in the living room. Sarala Khaling recalled, 'He used to love gin and tonic; and his latest craze was limoncello—an Italian drink with lemon peel and vodka and sugar.' He stocked all these in the bar, and whisky, Irish Cream, Kahlua, cognac. Moving out of his apartment in Mingma Norbu Sherpa's house was quite an ordeal, said Hira Kaji. 'It took two days just to move his books. And his clothes—he had so many! He gave them away to the workers, and even to the contractor.'

Both of Chandra's parents had passed on by the time the house was built. They never saw him properly settled.

Krishnakumari had died first, in 1995; and ten years later—a little more than a year before Chandra's death—the last mukhiya of Siklis village, Ratansingh, also passed away. Chandra had remained close to both till the end. Bandana Yonzon Lepcha told me that he frequently invoked his father at WWF meetings: 'He'd tell us, "My father had two sayings. One was: A tree that has a lot of fruit bends low. The other was: Those who are vocal can sell even flour; but those who stay silent can't sell even rice." He'd tell us this at every function, every gathering. He'd say, "That's what my father said."'

Yet as Chandra's stature had risen, he had had less time to visit Siklis. In Pokhara, his sister Humkali told me, 'Our parents always wanted him to stay longer when he went to the village. "Stay awhile," they would say. After he left, they'd wait for him to return, but...They'd ask him, "Is your work more important than we are?"'

When their parents were on their deathbeds, Chandra made sure they were taken care of, organizing their medical care and dispatching relatives to look after them. 'Of course, he told everyone what to do,' said Humkali, 'but he never had much time himself. He'd come, stay a while, then be off to meet someone. Sometimes he'd only phone; other times he'd come and stay, but only for a night,' she said. 'I'd tell him to stay longer, but he'd answer, "I have a lot of work to do, Didi." I'd caution him, I'd say don't travel when it rains, don't travel when the weather is foggy, but he wouldn't listen. He'd say he had a meeting at the office, and he'd go back to Kathmandu. He wouldn't even stay at home on Saturdays,' she said. 'He'd say, "I'll be right back," and he'd go out.'

For by then, Chandra had become the 'big person' his parents had always intended him to be. At heart still a boy from Siklis, his own power seemed to surprise him at the end of his life. His nephew Krishnaman Gurung recounted a phone call Chandra received when he was by his father's bedside at the hospital in Pokhara. Prime Minister Girija Prasad Koirala was on the line. 'His relative needed a job,' Krishnaman recalled to me. The prime minister asked Chandra whether he could help out. After they hung up, Chandra marvelled at what had just happened: 'He kept laughing that someone like the prime minister should call him, asking him for help!'

For Krishnakumari and Ratansingh's funeral rites, the family observed strict Gurung tradition, complete with pajyu and khebri shamans. This was deliberate. Earlier, on Ratansingh's eighty-fourth birthday, the family had made the mistake—at least in Harka Gurung's view—of having Hindu priests perform prayers. Harka Gurung had berated the family for being 'Hinduized'. The janajati rights movement was in full sway. A vociferous debate was taking place among the Gurungs—the Tamu—about reclaiming their heritage. 'Dr Harka Gurung was strongly for animism and shamanism,' Tshering explained to me. Chandra, she said, vacillated between Hinduism and shamanism. He was also happy to bow before Buddhist shrines. 'He wasn't political about being a janajati,' she said. Harka Gurung was more particular: 'He just didn't approve.'

Gurung funeral rites start with a feast three days after death, include rituals for a week in the case of a woman, and nine days in the case of a man. The ceremonies culminate in a rite that releases the soul of the deceased. Afterwards, those who can afford it host an arghau, a feast, aimed as much at celebrating the person's life as at mourning its end. The arghau for both Krishnakumari and Ratansingh took place in Siklis. Chandra's family and friends gathered both times. His brother Totraman even flew in from the United States to be there.

Family and friends gathered from all over the world for the arghau of Siklis's last mukhiya. Sumitra Manandhar Gurung came as well. This was the only time Chandra argued with her publicly. According to those who were there, he was convinced that she had come only to take photographs, to disprove that they had ever got separated, should he launch a new divorce case. Angrily, Chandra demanded that she leave the arghau. 'All she wants is the photos,' he railed to his family and friends.

Otherwise, the ceremonies went well. The family spent six to seven hundred thousand rupees feasting the village. In his later years, Ratansingh had repeatedly said, 'I've eaten something at every house here, so you must feed everyone at my arghau.' The family honoured his wish.

Chandra lived alone in his house, with two dogs for company: a Tibetan mastiff and a mongrel that he got when he moved in. Jit Bahadur Sunuwar of WWF stayed over at the start, helping out with chores, till Chandra's personal secretary Prajana Waiba Pradhan hired a caretaker from an agency. Chandra's daughter Amanda and son Adhish spent a few nights at the house sometimes. His nephews and nieces were also often there, visiting. 'He was very close to them,' recalled Hira Kaji Shrestha, 'almost closer than to his own children.' A cook came in for parties and special events. This was Chandra's home life, a lonely home life lacking an emotional core: a wife.

Tokiko Sato never moved to Nepal, and Chandra did not want to live anywhere else. Chandra's family and friends told me that towards the end there was some talk of their getting divorced. Relatives—who found it painful to see Chandra alone—urged him, in the Nepali way (with no consideration for the legalities), to find another wife, a proper Gurung-seni this time, who would care for him in old age. They even offered to set up a match, an offer he did not take up.

He lived alone till the end. But—a relentlessly social creature—he rarely spent a solitary evening. 'He could never be by himself, he always needed people around,' Dibya Gurung told me. He often invited members of his core group around. 'We would have potlucks, we would go to the movies. He wanted us to always stay together,' she said. 'He kept trying to get us to meet as a group.' She added, 'Sometimes it was too much.' Not all members of this group felt fondly towards each other. And, as Ghana Shyam Gurung (Ghurmet) said, 'We weren't like him, you know, we had our own families at home.'

Chandra also invited friends—of whom he had literally hundreds—to the house. He was constantly hosting parties. 'There was a set menu for drinks and snacks,' said Prajana Waiba Pradhan. 'If dinner was to follow, they would cater—his gatherings usually had twenty, twenty-two people.' Harka

Gurung and Tirtha Man Maskey were regulars at his parties, as were donors, government officials, army officers, childhood friends, development experts, academics, golf-course acquaintances, friends visiting from abroad...His social network was vast.

He also escaped the loneliness of his home through the company of colleagues at WWF. 'He loved sports, he loved music,' said Jit Bahadur Sunuwar. Chandra followed every trend, every fad: he bought an Ab King Pro to keep fit, Jit Bahadur said. 'He loved the cinema. He was always asking if anyone wanted to go to the cinema, and putting together groups of seven, eight people to go. If anyone ever recommended a film to him, he'd see it within three days.'

Sarala Khaling confirmed this. 'He once got upset at us because some of us went and saw a movie without him.' But when colleagues did take him to see a film, he could not follow the story. 'It was a real Bombay film, with typical street humour,' she said. Chandra did not understand Hindi. 'He'd fall asleep, then wake up and ask what's going on, what does that mean, what are they saying?'

When anyone at the office had anything to celebrate—personal or professional—he would send a box of sweetmeats through the office. He loved to gossip, and kept up with all the goings-on in everyone's personal life. Then he would tell everyone else about it. 'You couldn't tell him anything indiscreet,' recalled Dibya. 'He couldn't help it; he'd go and tell everyone—oh, have you heard what's going on with so-and-so?'

He would also round up the staff to go to restaurants. Bandana Yonzon Lepcha remembered, 'He loved going out to eat, he even loved going to discos. There was this one time he took everyone to the Rox, at the Hyatt.' Sarala Khaling described her surprise when Chandra suggested once that the staff go with him to a dance restaurant. Dance restaurants can be seedy dens of prostitution, but are not always so. Chandra's cousin, Badri Gurung, ran one of Kathmandu's largest dance restaurants, the Royal Kitchen. Chandra used to take Harka Gurung and Tirtha Man Maskey there from time to time. One day at the office, he turned to Sarala and suggested they go to his cousin's dance restaurant. 'I called home and told my family about it,' she laughed, recalling the discomfiture she had felt. She, Yeshi Choden Lama and Jennifer Headley—all close friends—went with Chandra to the Royal Kitchen. 'There wasn't anything bad about the place. There were just dance troupes,' said Sarala. At one point, Chandra remarked about a dancer, 'Eh, isn't she pretty?' 'It was—odd,' Sarala said, laughing.

It was the restlessness of a man with no home life. Chandra made the best of his social network, to be sure. But there was no one to turn to when something went wrong. Hira Kaji told me of an incident just a year before his death. 'It was in June/July, around then,' he said. 'Dr Sah'b was at home. He ate some fish and got a bone stuck in his throat. He phoned me, and I went over on my motorbike.' He drove Chandra to the emergency room of a private nursing home in the Thapathali neighbourhood. 'A doctor X-rayed him and said come tomorrow at five in the morning. So at four the next morning, I took him back to the hospital. They had to do an operation. I had to sign as the responsible person for him,' Hira Kaji said. 'That paper where they say that if anything should happen to him, I'll be responsible? There was no one else, so I signed it,' he said. It took an hour's operation to have the bone removed. Said Hira Kaji, 'They had put him out, he had been unconscious. But he didn't tell anyone about it, not even his children.'

Several people told me that in hindsight they felt that Chandra was unusually tense towards the end. 'I often asked him, are you okay?' Prajana told me. Bandana seconded this. 'He seemed—tired—in the last few months.' She told me that Tokiko had been hospitalized with a back injury. 'Something seemed wrong in his personal life,' she said. 'He was supposed to go to Jordan to meet his wife, but she went to Japan, to meet her mother. So he wasn't going to his wife. And she wasn't coming here either…'

Dibya recounted a rare instance, towards the end, in which she had seen Chandra drunk. 'He had a party in his house, and I guess he had had too much to drink,' she said. 'He got a bit—unruly. Saying—"Eh, it looks like I'll have to get married again."' Delicately, she said, 'I'd never seen him like that. He seemed to be under a lot of strain.'

KCAP's handover was occupying much of his energy. 'It was so important to him,' Prajana told me. 'He was doing everything himself. He was even typing all the letters himself. Maybe the tension of the handover was getting to him. He had lost weight.'

Yet he was at the height of his professional powers. Bandana recalled that in his last year—though no one had known that it was to be his last year—Chandra had been sharp, he had been shining. 'He was at the zenith of everything,' she said. 'To me, now, it seems as though—from there, where could he have gone? He was like a candle burning out,' she said. 'So bright.'

BIOPHILIA

As I researched Chandra's life and times, it struck me that in all the time I had known him—even at ACAP—I had rarely seen him out in nature. We tend to think of conservation a bit romantically, as entailing excursions into the wilderness. Or we link it to the natural sciences. In reality it involves a tiresome amount of social mobilization, of dealing with people—from government officials to specialists to elected office bearers, all the way down to local leaders and ordinary villagers. This suited the ever-garrulous Chandra. He excelled at winning people over to the cause of conservation. But did he, himself, love nature? Was he filled with the mystical wonder at nature—what the environmentalist E. O. Wilson has called 'biophilia'—that we imagine suffuses the soul of a naturalist? 'He must have,' replied Ghana Shyam Gurung (Ghurmet), somewhat bemused, when I put this question to him. 'He must have loved nature; otherwise why would he have done all this work to save it?' Yet it was not in the wilderness, but among people that I see Chandra till the end, surrounded by people, caught, always, in the web of human society.

I had, myself, not progressed beyond a vague 'love of nature' in the course of researching Chandra's life and times. Although—as WWF's Tilak Dhakal had said to me, 'For

Dr Sah'b, it wasn't just about tigers, elephants, rhinos. Conservation had to be for people'—Chandra's life's work had ultimately been for nature. That was his legacy. Yet I found myself still wishing for knowledge about nature.

Of all the projects that Chandra had launched at WWF, the Tarai Arc Landscape project, or TAL, was the most ambitious. I decided to go and see the project as a way of gaining the knowledge I still wished for.

Talking to me about the project, WWF's Anil Manandhar said, 'No one believed it could be done.' TAL covered a massive cross-border area incorporating eleven existing nature reserves: the Parsa Wildlife Reserve, the Royal Chitwan National Park, the Royal Bardiya National Park and the Royal Shuklaphanta Wildlife Reserve in Nepal; and in India, the Valmikinagar Wildlife Sanctuary, the Katarniaghat Wildlife Sanctuary, the Dhudhwa National Park, the Kishanpur Wildlife Sanctuary, the Corbett National Park, the Sonandi Wildlife Sanctuary and the Rajaji National Park. TAL's broad aim was to create a wildlife corridor between these reserves.

Anil explained to me that the concept of landscape conservation emerged at a WWF meeting in Indonesia in 2000, over a discussion on tiger conservation. Though national parks and protected areas serve as important sanctuaries for tigers, their population is not ultimately viable in these fragmented habitats, he said. These 'ecological islands' just do not have an adequate vegetation base to sustain self-replacing populations of herbivores and carnivores: the genetic pools are too small to ensure healthy reproduction. Corralling wildlife into national parks and protected areas does not therefore guarantee their survival in the long run.

WWF was looking for ways to conserve areas complex enough to sustain biodiversity. This usually requires large areas, or landscapes. Anil told me that the first landscape project in South Asia was in southern India. 'If WWF hadn't started the Tarai Arc Landscape, all the work that had gone into saving rhinos and tigers in the tarai would have been lost,' he said. But Bhutan was competing for a landscape project in its vicinity. 'There's a lot of politics in conservation,' he said. Were Bhutan to launch a landscape project, funds would have likely been diverted away from a similar project in Nepal. In 1995, Anil and a former WWF staff, Ukesh Bhuju, started to lobby hard for TAL. The lobbying intensified after Chandra joined WWF; and in September 2000, WWF launched the project, even before obtaining formal government endorsement.

In his office, Anil showed me a map of the project area: an elongated area occupying more than half of the tarai in Nepal, as well as contiguous land in India. 'Seven million people live in the Nepali part,' he said. 'Eventually, it'll cover this entire belt.' He tapped the eastern half of the tarai. The project envisioned the entire Nepal tarai serving as a wildlife corridor one day, most crucially for the elephant, rhinoceros and tiger populations native to the area. Again, Anil tapped the map. 'There was nothing here,' he said, with pride. 'Now, look. All this is going to be a wildlife corridor.'

He arranged for me to travel through the project area with Dhan Rai, a TAL staff. Dhan was going from Kathmandu, all the way through the western tarai, to his office in Dhangadi, in far-west Nepal. He was an energetic forty-something—no-

nonsense, but also full of tales. Setting out from Kathmandu in an office car, he told me that the work at TAL had been difficult during the war. 'It once took me eleven days to get from Chitwan to Dhangadi,' he said. This was normally a long day's bus ride. The Maoists had called a two-month bandh—closure—of Bardiya District, he said. 'I started off on a bus from Chitwan, but it stopped at the border of Bardiya. All the passengers had to get off.' Unable to find a ride further west, he crossed the border to India, and caught a westbound train. He re-entered Nepal on a rikshaa. 'But the rikshaa driver didn't agree to go all the way' he said, 'so I also had to walk.' Finally, he was able to find a car to take him to his destination. 'Bus, train, rikshaa, foot, car! It's not like that any more. Work is much, much easier now that the war has ended.'

We crossed the pass out of Kathmandu valley, and before too long were making our way out of the midlands, along the transverse gorges formed by the Trisuli and Narayani rivers. The Mahabharat range, with its low valleys and mountains of uniform metamorphic rocks, soon fell away, and we entered the Churia range, with low, hog-back hills composed of alternating soft and hard strata. The alluvial plains of the tarai stretched to the south.

At the universal level, the workings of nature are simple enough. Life is but an interplay of the non-living and living parts of the earth. The non-living parts consist of energy (heat and light, both of which originate from the sun) and matter (pure elements such as carbon, hydrogen, oxygen, nitrogen and phosphorous, and their combinations; in short: air, water, and minerals). It is the availability (or lack) of energy and matter that sets the conditions for the living parts of the earth.

These living parts consist, first, of plants, which are known as 'producers' because they derive nutrients from the non-living parts, and provide food to other living parts. Then there are 'consumers'—animals, including microorganisms, which feed on plants and on each other. Herbivores are 'primary' consumers; carnivores that eat only herbivores are 'secondary' consumers; and carnivores that eat other carnivores are 'tertiary' consumers.

At the simplest level, then, life consists of the movement of energy (heat and light) and matter (air, water and minerals) into plants and animals. But there are also other laws at work in nature: the first and second laws of thermodynamics. The first states that the total amount of energy in the universe is constant; it never increases or decreases. But energy does convert from one form to another. Yet, because nature tends towards entropy, these conversions are invariably inefficient. This is the second law of thermodynamics. The classic example of this is that 100,000 million calories of the sun's energy are expended on the growth of a plant (via photosynthesis); 10,000 calories from the plant are transferred to a herbivore (as food); and 1,000 calories are transferred to a carnivore that eats the herbivore. This is why a large vegetation base is required to support large carnivores such as tigers—1,000,000 kilograms of vegetation is needed to support 100,000 kilograms of herbivores, which in turn can support only 10,000 kilograms of carnivores. Any viable ecosystem needs many more plants than herbivores, and many more herbivores than carnivores.

These universal laws play out through varied species mixes locally. In Nepal, so geologically varied is the land that the climate varies from valley to valley. Villages on the same longitude, separated by only a few hills or mountains, can have vastly different micro-climates. Much depends, too, on the aspect of the land. There are no uniform tree lines or snow lines in Nepal. Such variations give rise to corresponding variations in the country's species mixes. The *Nepal Biodiversity Resource Book* count claims that in fauna, the country has a recorded 181 mammal species, 844 bird species, 100 reptile species, forty-three amphibian species, 185 freshwater fish species and 635 butterfly species. In flora, there are a recorded 5,160 flower plant species and 1,120 non-flowering plant species in Nepal. Of course, neither flora nor fauna observe political boundaries. They occur, rather, in local ecosystems which WWF categorizes in two ways: as large 'biogeographic realms' and as smaller 'ecoregions'.

Biogeographic realms indicate the broadest boundaries of natural evolutionary patterns: there are only eight biogeographic realms on earth. Nepal falls at the meeting point of two of these: the Palaearctic and the Indo-Malayan realms. The Palaearctic realm stretches over all of Europe, all of Asia north of, and including, the Himalayan range, Northern Africa, and the northern and central parts of the Arabian peninsula. The Indo-Malayan realm stretches over South and Southeast Asia, and includes the southern regions of East Asia. The meeting of these two realms in Nepal leads to a rich mix of high-altitude meadows and scrubland, sub-alpine coniferous and broadleaf forests, and tropical and subtropical savannas, scrublands, and broadleaf and deciduous forests.

WWF breaks these large biogeographic realms further down into 'ecoregions', smaller units that are distinct in their assemblage of natural communities. There are 825 terrestrial ecoregions worldwide, and 450 freshwater and 229 coast and shelf marine ecoregions. Of these, 200 ecoregions—known as the Global 200—are considered especially distinct, which is to say, especially rich in biodiversity, and especially vital to save. Nepal has eleven ecoregions, four of which are among the Global 200.

Roughly, from north to south, the eleven ecoregions in Nepal are: two (western and eastern) Palaearctic Himalayan alpine shrub and meadows; two Indo-Malayan Himalayan subalpine coniferous forests; two Indo-Malayan Himalayan broadleaf forests; the Indo-Malayan Himalayan subtropical pine forests; the Indo-Malayan Himalayan subtropical broadleaf forests; the Indo-Malayan Tarai-Duar savanna and grasslands; and two (upper and lower) small areas of the Indo-Malayan Gangetic plains moist deciduous forests.

Our drive took us west, to Butwal in Palpa District, where the Churia hills meet the plains of the tarai. The drive along the hills was picturesque, along riverbanks, with a blue magpie flitting across the road and a migrant grey heron swooping through the sky. Dhan Rai told me that Butwal—a modest industrial town—disrupts the wildlife corridor in the tarai: elephants, rhinoceroses and tigers cannot skirt human settlement—fields, roads and houses—to the south of the town, or climb the hills to the north. Was this problem serious enough to deplete their populations, I asked. He shrugged. 'There's been no study on the local carrying capacity, really.'

He explained that though environmentalists viewed these animals as flagship species—'They need a lot to survive, so they're symptomatic'—there had been little study done on their exact needs.

I had been reading E. O. Wilson's autobiography, *Naturalist*, learning that as much as 90 per cent of the earth's living species remained unknown to science. As Wilson put it: 'We have characterized about 180,000 of the flowering plants identified thus far out of a likely 230,000 species still living, as well as a large majority of land vertebrates (amphibians, reptiles, birds, and mammals), enough to advance conservation science and practices. But of the "little things that run the world," whose roles in maintaining healthy ecosystems are also crucial to our existence, we still know shockingly little.'

I asked Dhan whether there had been any study done on the effect of human settlement—fertilizers and pesticides—on smaller life forms, like insects.

He laughed. 'There's been nothing like that, no. It'll be a while before we get to things like that.'

It was exceedingly difficult, he explained, to work on natural science in Nepal. In Dolpo, Dhan had assisted the specialist Rodney Jackson in a month-long survey of snow leopards. 'Snow leopards won't come to your doorstep, right. You have to go where they are,' he said, laughing. This was painstaking work. Few Nepali environmentalists were willing to make that kind of an effort, he said. 'Those who have the technical know-how don't want to work that hard.' He mentioned a few early studies, but said that there had been little follow-up in recent years. He laid the blame on Nepal's education system. 'There's very little stress on technical knowledge. They give you just enough knowledge to get a job,' he said. 'That's all the knowledge they give.'

With this knowledge it was possible to do an impressive amount of work, I saw in the following days as I tagged along with Dhan. As at ACAP, the TAL staff worked closely with the local people, helping to improve their standards of living, to lessen their demands for natural resources and to avoid conflicts with the wildlife. So much was there to do in the villages, towns and cities of the project area, the staff got hardly any opportunity at all to be in nature.

That night, in an airless, concrete-walled hotel room in Butwal, Dhan met Amar Singh Pradhan, who headed a coordination committee of thirty community forest user groups in nearby Dovan. TAL found it expedient to work through such coordination committees, I learned. These committees, in turn, made it easier for the local people to trust TAL. 'At the start,' Amar Singh Pradhan said to me, 'when there was talk about turning this area into a wildlife corridor, people thought everyone would be moved away to make room for bears and tigers. It was only later that we understood.' Echoing Chandra's words, he explained, 'You can't start off telling people to conserve their forests. They just won't listen. But if you do things that benefit them, they'll trust you, they'll say, "this organization does good work"—and they'll start to heed you. They'll do what you want after that.'

The next morning, we went to Dovan, a settlement at the confluence of the Jhumsa and Tinau rivers. There, Dhan met with Motilal Lamsal, a member of a local CFUG. In Motilal's kitchen, his wife was cooking the morning meal on an 'improved stove', so called because it uses less firewood than traditional stoves. It also eliminated indoor smoke. Women's health improved with it. Children could study by the hearth. Eighty per cent of Dovan's houses had installed such stoves after TAL helped to train local 'promoters', who earned a small income—eighty or hundred or up to 140 rupees—on each stove that they built. Nevertheless, the construction of new stoves had petered out, because all the promoters had left the village. Motilal was hoping that TAL would train a new batch of promoters. 'We need new promoters here,' he said to Dhan.

Afterwards we stood awhile by his house, looking north, towards the confluence. A lone fisherman was standing on a wooden bridge above the Tinau River. Till a few years earlier, people used to use poison to catch fish here, Dhan told me. With TAL's guidance the village had now banned this practice. The fish populations had revived, and the local species—'asala, thed, rahu, sahar, kavre, butuna'—had burgeoned. 'They come right up to the surface of the water now. Just at the river's surface—they're all right there.'

The forest surrounding Dovan, too, was regenerating slowly. It was sparse, but it had been sparser still in the mid 1990s, Motilal said. With the advent of community forestry, the village had been able to manage the forests itself, which proved more effective. 'We realized that we could save the forests if we just prevented theft by outsiders. As for us, we get by with whatever falls naturally.' The CFUGs also banned the use of axes. 'Anything we cut has to be small enough to be cut with a sickle,' Motilal said. An additional rule against cutting 'wet', or green, wood helped to reverse the previous decades' deforestation.

Dhan pointed at a tree on the far shore of the river, a grand old tree towering over the others. It was, he said, the 'mother tree' of a rare species of sal, called bijaya sal. 'There's a belief that its wood purifies water. It turns the water a kind of blue-red,' he said. 'People say it has medicinal properties.' The village was protecting the mother tree, as its seeds were needed to grow new trees. It hoped to harvest its wood one day. This was just one of the rare species native to these forests, Dhan told me, rattling off a list of others: serpentine root, Himalayan coral bean, satti sal.

There was no time to tarry, however, as Dhan's work in Dovan was done, and we had to be on our way to his next appointment. On the westward drive, Dhan told me, cheerfully, that the people of the area were sighting kalij pheasants by their houses now. 'They didn't use to, before. There are also lots of minivets migrating to Siberia through here now. There's been a visible regeneration of wildlife,' he said, adding, with dark humour, 'You even see more roadkill on the highway than you used to.'

Then he told me about the many initiatives that TAL had started in the vicinity: Eco-clubs in the schools, loans to women's groups to support goat rearing and vegetable farming, thus increasing the local standard of living. He spoke of a trial in farming long pepper, a local variety of what foresters call 'non-timber species'. 'Farming it didn't work in the fields, but it worked in the forests.' Harvesting it would bring an income eventually. He discussed local biogas plants—some successful, others less so—and solar energy schemes. He also talked about two micro-hydro projects that TAL had helped build, in nearby Purwan Khola and Suketal. The former scheme offered the cheapest electricity in Nepal: 'Seventy-five paisa per unit!' The latter scheme was built in a Dalit village. 'We gave money for the machinery, and the rest of the expense was raised by the villagers,' he said. 'When the village lit up, it was like a challenge to other villages—if they can light up their corner, why can't we?'

Dhan reminded me completely of my former colleagues at ACAP, with his intimate knowledge of the project area, his feel for its people—and his tirelessness. That afternoon we drove straight through to the town of Lamahi, in Dang District, one of the key settlements of the Tharus, the indigenous people of the tarai. Dhan told me that the low-lying valleys here formed a 'bottleneck' in the wildlife corridor: elephants, rhinoceroses, and tigers had to take a narrow passage east or west through here. Inevitably, they came into contact with humans, sometimes disastrously. Two wild elephants had recently died here after becoming entangled in electrical wires.

In the office of the coordination committee of twenty-three local CFUGs, Dhan met with Kiran Bhandari, a committee member. They discussed the need for more active forest management, the market possibilities for herb and vegetable farming, and the merits of managed plotting in the forests. Overgrazing was a serious problem; they discussed ways by which the coordination committee might prevent it. The coordination committee had enough funds to promote biogas plants in the houses, and to establish a 'wildlife insurance fund' out of which cattle owners could be compensated when their cattle were killed by bears or leopards or wild boar. The committee had trained 'Aadhiya'—Tharu leaders—in conservation, I learned. They had taught local cow herders methods to prevent overgrazing. They had started eighteen eco-clubs in the vicinity. They had passed rules about forest use, enforcing fines. They were now worrying over ways to increase income locally—offering loans of twenty-five thousand rupees to small businesses to make tapari leaf-plates, or rasari ropes. The coordination committee here was clearly ambitious. 'We want to register as a cooperative,' Kiran said to Dhan. 'That way, we can give out loans ourselves. We wouldn't need to turn to donor agencies.'

I grew tired just listening.

Afterwards, Kiran talked to me awhile. The local CFUGs, I learned, had already been in place when TAL started up here. 'We were already working in TAL's style,' he said, when Chandra had shown up. 'He had a different vision,' Kiran said. The committee's work had expanded dramatically after partnering up with TAL.

Yet, during the war, TAL had had to stay in the background, allowing the coordination committee to take the lead locally. This, because the Maoists opposed projects with American funding. Not wanting to put the coordination committee's work at risk, TAL had all but erased its own presence during the war. 'Everyone just thought—the coordination committee does good work,' Kiran explained to me, laughing. 'Now, of course, it's different. We've started to be open about the partnership. But during the war,' he said, laughing again, 'people thought it was just the coordination committee doing all this work!'

Soon we were on our way again, driving through a picturesque stretch buffeted on both sides by grassy cliffs. Dhan recalled that during the war, the Maoists had ambushed an Armed Police convoy here, in Kusum. 'The convoy was heading to the Sumsheregunj barracks. The Maoists were up there'—he pointed at the cliffs—'and they shot from both sides. They killed six people in the convoy. After that, for six months, you couldn't drive through here at all, the security was so tight.'

Further along, we entered a densely forested stretch that the then prime minister, Girija Prasad Koirala, had pledged as a 'Gift to the Planet' at the WWF gala that Chandra had organized in 2000. The plan, then, had been to extend the Bardiya National Park, which was nearby, all the way here. Dhan said, 'But the plan was stopped when the army asked for a budget to manage it. The plan just vanished after that!'

The forests thinned as we neared the town of Nepalgunj, where we were to lodge for the night. Concrete houses began to crop up in the small highway towns, towering over the more traditional huts and hovels. Large numbers of bicyclists were heading into town, their baskets stacked high with firewood. Dhan explained to me that each of these bicyclists would have spent the day gathering the firewood that they would now sell in Nepalgunj. We passed ten, fifteen, then scores of such bicyclists. 'That's how they make their living,' Dhan said.

But where I saw deforesters, Dhan saw potential environmentalists. 'These people,' he said, 'what we should do is, make them give speeches on the importance of forests. Each one of them.' They, more than anyone, knew how easy it used to be to find firewood here, he explained. 'They know how hard it is now. They understand the value of conservation more than anyone else,' he said. 'They know how much easier life would be if their forests were nice and dense!'

That night, in a hotel room in Nepalgunj, I mused over how little time one spent out in nature when doing conservation work. It was all people, people, people. That was how it had been at ACAP. That was how it was at TAL.

AFTER THE STORM

The next morning, again, we were off to meetings, one after another, all along our westward drive.

Our first stop was by a forest called the 'Thulo ban'—the large forest—by the edge of the Bardiya National Park. TAL had helped to open up a bel-juice plant here. Bel is a variety of quince, Bengal quince, native to this area. The juice plant was in a concrete house. Dhan talked awhile to the operator, a local man, a Dalit. He showed us the room where the fruit was being crushed, juiced and bottled. The operator, of course, benefited from sales of the juice in supermarkets in distant Kathmandu. The local staff got employment. And each local fruit collector earned Rs 2 for a bushel of bel fruit, of which Re 1 went to a community fund. 'Everyone benefits, and there's no harm to the forests,' the operator boasted. Then he offered us a glass each of fresh juice. 'There's no sugar added—it's suitable even for diabetics!'

In the midday heat, the juice was thoroughly refreshing.

We then made our way south, into the inner tarai—a largely undeveloped stretch along the border with India, criss-crossed only by rough mud tracks. Here, there were no concrete houses, just huts and hovels. Government presence grew very sparse. The mud tracks led to the Karnali River. Dolphins—

Ganges River dolphins—were still found in the river, despite development, overfishing and the construction of bridges, ferries and irrigation canals. From the shore, we caught a quick, dark splash in the calm brown surface of the river. Then we saw it again. And again. Dolphins—four, maybe five—kept popping up by turns.

We took a floating bridge across the river, and on the far shore, drove through more mud tracks to eventually reach the Tharu village of Khata.

There, Dhan met the members of the coordination committee of the local CFUGs, a committee that consisted, as its members good-naturedly told me, of a chairman who had only one eye, a deaf secretary and a blind accountant. 'And our previous chairman didn't have any legs,' one man exclaimed, to much hilarity.

I was, to be honest, fatigued by then. It had taken so much of an effort to reach this single village—in so vast a project area. But, as I remembered well from ACAP, there is little reprieve for field staff like Dhan; and so there was little reprieve for me as he discussed work with the committee members.

The work centred on asparagus farming, lemongrass and chamomile farming, and the processing of mint. It also focused on preventing conflicts between people and wildlife.

The present chairman of the committee, Bhadai Tharu, had lost his eye in a tiger mauling, I learned. He and other villagers had been collecting grass. 'We formed a circle—not intentionally, it just happened that way,' he explained to me after the committee's work was done. A tiger was trapped in the middle. Trying to escape, it struck Bhadai, tearing off half his face. Doctors at a hospital in Nepalgunj had just barely managed to repair his face. 'And yet—look. I'm trying to save tigers!' he laughed.

It struck me as remarkable.

'And it's working,' he continued. 'The animal population has increased here. Wild elephants come by every summer, and raid the villagers' corn fields.' To prevent this, the committee had helped to build trenches around the village fields, trenches that the elephants were unable to cross. The committee had also helped to build machaans—lookouts—from where the villagers could keep vigil each night. 'The border is right there,' Bhadai said, meaning the border with India, where the elephant populations were larger. 'It's impossible to keep animals from coming and going through the village. But if we can see them coming, we can at least scare them away.'

'How does one scare away wild elephants?' I asked.

One of the committee members said, 'We light fires, we make loud noises. Everyone from the village gets up and causes a commotion. Banging together pots and pans, anything.'

'All of you keep vigil yourselves?'

The villagers, they explained, took turns.

Bhadai said, 'Now, when the elephants come, there's nothing they can eat, so they go away.' There was a nearby forest with plenty of sugar cane, he said. 'It's nicer for them there, so they go there.'

All this had happened with help from TAL. Talking to the committee members, I was struck by how the project had converted ordinary villagers into environmentalists. Bhadai Tharu, I learned, had spent seventeen years as a kamaiya—a hereditary bonded labourer, akin to a slave—to a wealthy landowner. As a kamaiya, he used to organize hunts for the landowner's family. 'They'd have guests from outside—foreigners—and I'd have to tell them where the spotted deer were,' Bhadai recalled, laughing. 'How could I have known any better? They'd kill truckfuls of spotted deer—and I'd help them!'

He won his independence from the family after the kamaiya liberation movement of 2000. As a free man, Bhadai had come to take an interest in conservation—not out of a love of nature, but because he saw some benefit in it.

'Look, the grass in our community forests is free,' he said. 'Whereas it costs a lot if you have to buy it.' And there was an income to be earned from the farming of asparagus, lemongrass, chamomile and mint...

Still, it seemed to me that the committee was doing more than what was to the village's immediate benefit.

Bhadai admitted it, adding ruefully that indeed there was little thanks for conservation work. 'Every time there's a problem with an elephant or a rhinoceros, the villagers say—look at what your animals have done,' he said, 'as though the animals belong to us!' Nevertheless, the committee had soldiered on, launching a health clinic to win local support for their work, and also establishing a 'livestock insurance' fund out of which they compensated those whose cattle were killed by wild animals. The committee had even formed an anti-poaching team.

This team consisted of one member from each local CFUG. 'Tiger parts are profitable: poachers earn two or three hundred thousand rupees from each tiger,' Bhadai said. Rhinoceros poachers tended to poison the animals before killing them.

Though the anti-poaching team had no legal authority to punish poachers, they could, and did, report poachers to the government District Forest Office. Most of the poachers were from elsewhere, Bhadai said, but occasionally, a local villager would give in to the temptation. 'It's very hard to teach people about right and wrong,' he said, shaking his head. 'Herding cows is easy by comparison!' He laughed. 'It's nowhere as easy to herd people!'

We took leave of the committee members and resumed our journey along the mud tracks, butterflies fluttering out of the forests: big, black, flappy-winged butterflies with pale spots. Swallowtails. It was their season of flight.

Eventually we reached the highway. Not far along, in the small town of Ghodaghodi, Dhan met with members of a youth club that had been working to save the turtles, fish and alligators in a nearby lake. The club had also established an anti-poaching team, and they wanted TAL to provide them with torches: a meagre expense. They talked to Dhan about two bird surveys that they had conducted, and about the hundreds of fishing hooks they had convinced villagers to hand over. Someone passed around a jar containing the carcass of a snake, a poisonous species locally called a mahiya, white with black spots, coiled now in formaldehyde. One man talked, wishfully, of the possibility of a telephone hotline for farmers, to ask about such matters as chemical fertilizers and pesticides. 'They have a place like that in India, Pantnagar,' he said. 'It's like—a university for farmers. If only we could have something like that in our own Nepal! How helpful that would be!'

I had nothing but respect for Dhan, whose energy seemed never to flag during these meetings. His feel for the project area, and its people, was genuine. As we resumed our journey along the highway, he chatted on amicably about a local delicacy, musako achaar—pickled mice. 'In all the village fairs, that's the first item that sells out. It's so tasty, I love it!' We passed a stretch of the highway where, during the war, a human head had once been found, impaled on a stick. 'Things were bad, things were bad,' he said, sighing. About Chandra, he joked: 'A clever man! He'd invite all those donors and diplomats home, and serve them booze, and they'd feel so good they'd say yes to anything. Then—what to do? The next day, they'd have to approve funds for his projects.'

Nearing nightfall we reached the town of Dhangadi, in Kailali District, where Dhan worked out of a WWF branch office. We found the town in tumult. We learned that some Maoist cadres had been killed, a few days before, in nearby Bardiya District. Though the Maoists were in government, cadres of their ethnic Tharu wing—the Tharuwan Liberation Front—had called a bandh that day. When the police tried to prevent the closure from being enforced, a violent clash had erupted. Forty-five people had been wounded. The assistant chief district officer had sustained a head injury. He—with a conspicuously bandaged head—was being evacuated to Kathmandu on the last flight out that day, along with the chief district officer. We ran into them at the hotel where I was to stay. All the government offices in town were shut. The atmosphere was besieged.

When I went to take leave of Dhan the next morning, I found the front door of WWF branch office locked. The Tharuwan

Liberation Front had called another bandh that day. Entering from a back door, I found Dhan and the other staff working inside, but discreetly. Not wishing to disturb them, I thanked Dhan and left.

I had decided to spend that day, my last, visiting the Shuklaphanta Wildlife Reserve. This reserve, in the very south-west tip of Nepal, shared physical similarities with the Dudhwa National Park, immediately across the border, in India. Both fell in the Indo-Malayan Tarai-Duar savanna and grasslands ecoregion, with rare, tall grasslands that housed Asia's highest densities of tigers, rhinoceroses and ungulates. This ecoregion was on the Global 200 list. I also wanted, finally, to be out in nature, to be free, awhile, of people, people, people. As one of Nepal's oldest reserves, Shuklaphanta also offered a sense of what the tarai was like before its settlement and present-day depletion. This was what I wanted to see.

It was not easy to do. The town of Mahendranagar (originally named after King Mahendra, and since renamed Bhim Dutta) was also under the Tharuwan Liberation Front bandh that day. The highway into town was blockaded. The driver had to take a tortuous side-road through dusty farmlands. A long drive later, we reached the far end of the town. There, by the office of Shuklaphanta's chief warden, was the entrance to the reserve.

The chief warden was not in his office.

Nor was the assistant warden in his.

So I waited outside their offices, learning, from an aged grounds-minder, that the Tharuwan Liberation Front's cadres had padlocked the District Forest Office in town. The Chief

Warden had gone to help out, he told me. 'He should be back in a while.'

Almost two hours later, he was not back. The minder dispatched a peon to find him, to no avail. Finally, the driver and I drove into town, only to find the District Forest Office padlocked, indeed. There were no government officials to be found anywhere. Though Mahendranagar was the centre of Kanchanpur District, it turned out to be a squalid bazaar with only one street to speak of. We had a dal-bhat meal at a flyblown restaurant and returned to the entrance of the reserve, hoping the chief warden was back.

He was not.

'Can't we go into the reserve without talking to him?' I asked the minder.

'It would be good if you could talk to him,' he said.

'But do we have to?' I persisted.

'It would be good,' he said.

I sighed, I waited. The afternoon wore on. My hopes dimmed.

Then the sky suddenly darkened. Out of nowhere, a storm descended. One moment the sky had been clear; the next moment, a fierce wind was whipping down, bending and shaking the trees. Leaves and branches flew up, the underbrush sashayed madly. A low howl rose from the land. Dust flew up from the ground, turning the sky an eerie yellow-brown.

The minder scuttled about shuttering the office doors and windows. Storm clouds manifested overhead. Then came the rains, a sudden, shocking roar of water pummelling the land.

The pummelling lasted barely ten minutes. Then, just as abruptly as it had started, the storm ended. The rain ceased. The clouds evaporated. The sky cleared.

'It's always like that,' the minder remarked gaily as the sun emerged over a scrubbed and gleaming land. 'If there's a wind first, the rain doesn't last. It's always like that in this season.'

By then it was past three o'clock. I figured I was out of luck. 'It doesn't look like the chief warden is coming, does it?' I asked the minder.

'No, it doesn't,' he agreed.

'And can't we go in otherwise?' I asked.

'Yes, you can,' he said.

'I can?'

'You can. Better not to wait too long. Come. Let's go,' he said, hopping into the car with the driver and me.

So grateful was I for this unexpected turn of events, I did not question his earlier refusal. To my delight, the minder proved very knowledgeable about the reserve. 'There used to be only one rhino here, it came from the Indian side,' he said as we headed in past the towering sal trees, past the entrance. I had never seen sal trees this big; I had never even realized they could grow so tall. In an effort to create viable populations through the tarai, the Department of National Parks and Wildlife Conservation had, in 2003, translocated six rhinoceroses here. Two had died of disease, the minder told me. 'But two babies were born, so there's still the same number of rhinos. The new don't stray very far. The local rhino, it knows its way throughout the reserve,' he said. 'But the rhinos they brought in from outside, they stay where the helicopter put them down. I guess they just haven't got their bearings.'

Deeper in, the sal forest gave way to a rich mix of silk cotton, cutch and redwood trees, all dappled with light, moisture dripping from their leaves, from the storm. Now and again we stopped at a clearing, sighting spotted deer and antelope in the undergrowth. 'The horns have just fallen off, this is the season when they fall off,' the minder whispered about an antelope, called barasinghe, or 'the twelve-horned', in Nepali.

The trees eventually gave way to grasslands teeming with the tall narenga, or elephant grass. The car was easily dwarfed by the elephant grass. The storm had caused a tree to fall across the track; we had to clear it to pass by. At the southern end of the reserve we reached a savanna, a vast, rustling plain, one of the very rare savannas of Nepal.

We got out of the car and climbed atop a machaan. A thousands-strong herd of swamp deer was feeding on the savanna, the elegant russet creatures hunched over, oblivious to our presence.

From the vantage point of the machaan, we could see all the way to the Churia range in the north. In all other directions, the land was covered with grasses, with shrubs, with trees, as far as the eye could see. The winds shifted. The plains swayed. The swamp deer kept feeding, oblivious. It was an impossible idyll.

We climbed down from the machaan and returned to the car. As we continued, past the lotus ponds and the swamplands, I found myself wishing that other parts of the tarai, other parts of the country—even cities as debased as Kathmandu—could be reinvested with the magic, the mystery, that was in this reserve. I knew better than to think this an easy task. Yet I wished we could live, daily, with the beauty that is present in a national park or reserve.

I thought of the old-growth rhododendron forests beyond Siklis, how beautiful they had been. I thought of the breaking of the monsoon in Pokhara—how it had taken me by surprise. How we limit ourselves in the confines of human society. I thought of all the—people, people, people—that TAL's work entailed. That was as it should be, I reminded myself. In the democratic, and even radical, milieu of the day, conservation work had to involve people centrally, and to benefit them. And indeed, people are not separate from nature. I had to check my own romanticism—the mistaken view that nature is 'out there', pristine. I had to remind myself that nature is the depleted settlements we live in, where conservation work must of necessity concentrate.

Then I looked around me, at the idyll, and thought: there is at least this. There is at least this idyll to remind us of what we have lost, to show us what we might regain, because of the work environmentalists had done in the past. At the edges of the reserve, I took in the towering sal trees, and I thought, with gratitude, of all the work that environmentalists had done, and were doing, for our land, for us. I thought of Chandra. I thought of the generations that had preceded him, and the generations that would follow, all the lives given up— for this. They lived on here. This was their afterlife.

We reached a clearing in the sal trees. Out of the stillness came a sudden fleeting. A spotted deer bounded past us, and stopped, turned, looked at us, then bounded away, gracefully, into the undergrowth. I thought of Chandra and I watched it go.

ACKNOWLEDGEMENTS

My profound thanks to Ravi Singh for his interest in stories from far-flung corners. Thank you to Jaishree Ram Mohan for her skilful editing. I would like to thank everyone at the Chandra Gurung Conservation Foundation and the World Wildlife Fund Nepal for their help in writing this biography, and particularly Anil Manandhar, Ghana Shyam Gurung (Ghurmet), Shailendra Thakali, Bandana Yonzon Lepcha, Prajana Waiba Pradhan, as well as all the staff at the Annapurna Conservation Area Project and the National Trust for Nature Conservation, who so respected Dr Sah'b—as they, and also I, called Chandra Gurung. I have named everyone who agreed to be interviewed in the text. I have also quoted, with due acknowledgement, from Hum Bahadur Gurung's excellent interview of Chandra, and from innumerable WWF Nepal publications before and after his death. My thanks to the authors of these documents. I would like to thank everyone else—from Siklis to Pokhara to Kathmandu to China, Australia, the United Kingdom and the United States—who shared their knowledge of and feelings for Chandra. Judith Amtzis's keen editing proved helpful in the early drafts, as did General Sir Sam Cowan's archival knowledge of Nepal. I would also like to thank Chandra's family, especially Dr Sumitra Manandhar Gurung, Amanda Manandhar Gurung, Adhish

Manandhar Gurung, Dr Tokiko Sato, Humkali Gurung, Dr Totraman Gurung, Major Hitman Gurung, Krishnaman Gurung and Lokraj Gurung, who were big-hearted, generous and wise through their grief. Thanks always to my parents, Bhekh B. Thapa and Rita Thapa, to my siblings (and sibling-in-law) Bhaskar and Sumira and Tej Thapa, and my partner Daniel Lak, for their support.

I relied on much existing literature for my research, in particular: Toni Hagen's *Nepal*; Oleg Polunin and Adam Stainton's *Concise Flowers of the Himalaya*; Robert L. Fleming, Sr, Robert L. Fleming, Jr and Lain Singh Bangdel's *Birds of Nepal*; Richard Grimmett and Carol and Tim Inskipp's *Birds of Nepal*; Colin Smith's *Butterflies of Nepal*; 'Gurungs and Gurkhas' by Dorothy Mierow, in pokharacity.com; 'Effectiveness of Community Involvement in Delivering Conservation Benefits to the Annapurna Conservation Area, Nepal' by Siddhartha B. Bajracharya, Peter A. Furley and Adrian C. Newton, in *Environmental Conservation*, 2005; the colourful and informative memoir *The Soul of the Rhino* by Hemanta Mishra; *Tiger Warden*, Laxmibadan Maskey's moving memoir of her life with Tirtha Man Maskey; *Pokhara: Biography of a Town* by Jagannath Adhikari and David Seddon; 'Kings as Wardens and Wardens as Kings: Post-Rana Ties between Nepali Royalty and National Park Staff' by Nina Bhatt, in *Conservation and Society*; 'Luxury and Comfort Marked King's Hunt' in *The New York Times*; 'Hapless Hunting' in *Time*; *Nepal Community Forestry 2005*, by Keshav Raj Kanel, Ram Prasad Poudyal and Jagadish Prasad Baral; 'After the King, It's the Maoists' by Kiran Nepal, with Yogesh Dhakal and Dewan Rai, in *Himal Khabarpatrika*, 14-28 March 2008; 'King Has Shares in

17 Companies', in *The Kathmandu Post*, 27 August 2008; and studies and reports by the World Wildlife Fund, especially *WWF in Nepal: Three Decades of Partnership in Conservation (1967-2000)*, which offers an overview of the history of conservation in Nepal; and reports by the National Trust for Nature Conservation, the International Centre for Integrated Mountain Development (ICIMOD), the International Union for the Conservation of Nature, the Nature Conservancy and Conservation International. *Nepal Biodiversity Resource Book*, jointly published by the ICIMOD, the Government of Nepal, the United Nations Environment Programme and nepalnature.com, proved a crucial document. I have also been informed by Rachel Carson's *A Sense of Wonder*; E. O. Wilson's *Naturalist*; and all of Jared Diamond's books, including *Collapse*.

The Chandra Gurung Conservation Foundation was established by friends and followers of Chandra Gurung to maintain his legacy. All my proceeds from this publication will go to the foundation for conservation work in Nepal.